HISTORY FILES   The Cold War

The Cold War

MICHAEL F. HOPKINS

Thames & Hudson HISTORY FILES

HALF TITLE Poster celebrating the first Soviet atomic bomb explosion, 1949.
TITLE PAGES Man wielding a pickaxe to participate in the destruction of the Berlin Wall, 10 November 1989.
THIS PAGE President Kennedy meets US Army officials just after the Cuban missile crisis, November 1962.

First published in the United Kingdom in 2011 by Thames & Hudson Ltd, 181A High Holborn, London WC1V 7QX

British Library Cataloguing-in-Publication Data
A catalogue record for this book is available from the British Library

ISBN 978-0-500-28958-7

Printed in Hong Kong through Asia Pacific Offset Ltd

To find out about all our publications, please visit www.thamesandhudson.com. There you can subscribe to our e-newsletter, browse or download our current catalogues and buy any titles that are in print.

Contents

Introduction

Competing Worlds

The first half of the 20th century was dominated by two world wars, their unprecedented violence bringing nearly 60 million deaths. The second half of the century was dominated by the Cold War. As a complex historical development it is not easy to define, but its basic outline is plain enough. It was a geopolitical contest between the United States and its allies on one side and the Soviet Union and China and their associates on the other. It was typical of international relations since at least the 16th century in that it was about power: the strongest states competed on the international stage. In the early 20th century the great powers were Germany, Great Britain, France, Russia and, to a lesser extent, Italy, joined by the growing Japan. The economic power of the United States made it potentially a great power, but the political will and military might were absent for most of this period.

By 1945 Germany, Italy and Japan had been humbled. This left the Soviet Union (Russia's successor), the United States and the weakened Britain. Soon Britain and the United States were in disputes with the Soviet Union over the postwar settlement. What followed was geopolitical disagreement, military competition and the progressive expansion of the rivalry from Europe to Asia to Africa to Latin America. In this respect, events were typical of earlier episodes of great power tensions. But this was also an ideological struggle – between, on one side, Soviet Communism and, on the other, Western market economics and representative democracy (or capitalism, according to the Soviet explanation). It was a contest between

Soviet soldier hoisting the Soviet flag over the Reichstag in Berlin, May 1945.

OPPOSITE Aerial view of Hiroshima, Japan, eight months after the August 1945 atomic bombing.

different visions of politics and the world, and as such it was pursued not just by politicians and the military. It became a battle of ideas, supported by publicity and propaganda campaigns aimed at their own populations as well as those on the other side. The Bolshevik Revolution of 1917 and the emergence of the Soviet Union coincided with the rise of the era of mass politics and mass communications. Persuasion offensives targeted the masses through newspapers, radio and newsreels and later television.

Most histories of the Cold War have concentrated primarily on the political-strategic struggle. In the last two decades increasing attention has been paid to the battle of ideas, to the competition in propaganda, to the cultural Cold War, and most recently to the nature and development of Cold War culture. It was once assumed that all major cultural phenomena of the era could be attributed to the Cold War, but it has since become clear that there were other sources of inspiration as well. The years after 1945 saw two other developments. One was the unprecedented economic growth in the Western world from the 1940s to the 1970s, which was renewed in the 1990s. There was also a youth revolution that began in the West but soon made its impact felt across the generations and throughout the world.

Heroic depiction of the Communist revolution: Boris Kustodiev's *The Bolshevik* (1920).

This book examines the Cold War era by exploring how these various forces intersected. It does not attempt the task, impossible even in a much larger work, of offering a total history of the postwar era, but aims to chart the power-political and cultural arcs of the East-West conflict and identify its main developments. The central purpose is to consider the government policies of the primary protagonists on the main issues and to assess how the Cold War rivals sought to persuade both their adversaries and their own people. In this way it can try to capture a sense of the experience of the citizens caught up in the conflict. The main focus is on Western and Eastern Europe, the United States, the Soviet Union and China, although it will also look at the effect of Cold War rivalries on Africa, Latin America and the Middle East. Certain lines of explanation will be suggested, but the primary goal is to encourage further reflection.

American youth waiting to see the movie *Houdini* (1953).

Chapter 1

Origins: 1917–1945

In October 1917 Lenin and the Bolsheviks seized control of the seat of the Russian government and then fought for control of the state in a civil war that would last until 1921. In March 1918 the new Communist leaders signed the Treaty of Brest-Litovsk taking Russia out of the First World War. Anxious to keep Russia in the war, the Allies sent forces into Russia to aid the 'whites', who wished to continue fighting, in their civil war against the Bolshevik 'reds'. So began the antagonism between Communism and the West. This first phase of confrontation was short-lived, and by the end of 1919 most foreign forces had departed. After victory in the civil war, the Bolsheviks created the Soviet Union in 1922 with Lenin as its first leader. For nearly a decade and a half after 1919 the major Western states had limited contact with the Soviets. Under Republican presidents in the 1920s the United States turned away from active involvement in international affairs and pursued the expansion of American business interests. Because the Soviet Union refused to honour the debts of the previous tsarist regime, it became something of an international pariah. The two main protagonists of the future Cold War found few occasions to enter into conflict.

The rise of Communists to power had a more dramatic impact on the domestic politics of the United States and the major European powers. In 1918–19 there was a series of abortive revolutions in Germany, Austria and Hungary. Communist parties appeared in all the European countries and in the United States. The phenomenon

Badge depicting Lenin (Vladimir Ilyich Ulyanov).

OPPOSITE Portrait of Joseph Stalin in the Stalin Museum, Batumi, Georgia.

also emerged of the fellow-traveller, the officially non-Communist
sympathizer with Moscow. In Britain George Bernard Shaw, the cel-
ebrated playwright, was joined by the writers Sidney and Beatrice
Webb in praising what they described as the new Soviet civilization.
In the United States the journalist John Reed's heroic account of the

Charlotte and George
Bernard Shaw, seated
centre, with Sidney and
Beatrice Webb seated
either side, departing for
a trip to Russia, 1932.

The Appeal of Communism

After the 1917 Bolshevik Revolution, Communist parties appeared in all the European countries and in North America, attracting those who wanted to remove the social and economic inequities from their societies. Communism might have regarded itself as a movement of the working masses, but it rarely achieved mass appeal, although the German party polled 3–4 million votes in the 1920s. Most members were the most downtrodden of the working class, joined by a small group of middle-class intellectuals who became more prominent in the 1930s, as the appeal of Communism grew. In 1929–32, when capitalism seemed to be collapsing in the Great Depression, many turned to Communism as the only available economic solution. The Communist Party was also very effective in launching a popular front of the left against the threat of fascism, which boosted the membership.

Finally, there were those such as Burgess, Maclean and Philby in Britain and Ethel and Julius Rosenberg in the United States who spied for the Soviet Union. Their motivations were complex and varied but may have involved a mixture of devotion to Communism, the appeal of being engaged in something that set them apart and demonstrated their talents, and perhaps an attraction to illicit activities.

Communist propaganda poster: 'Freedom – American-style'.

Soviet poster celebrating the October Revolution and the Communist International, 1922.

Bolshevik Revolution, *Ten Days that Shook the World*, was published in 1919. Paul Robeson, the gifted black singer, said in 1935: 'From what I have already seen of the workings of the Soviet Government, I can only say that anybody who lifts his hand against it ought to be shot! It is the government's duty to put down any opposition to this really free society with a firm hand…. It is obvious that there is no terror here, that all the masses of every race are contented and support their government.'[1] The rise of outright support and widespread sympathy for Communism meant all Western security services were on the alert. US authorities, however, adopted an especially tough response. The Department of Justice detected a serious threat from Bolshevism, an impression reinforced by Lenin's letter to American

I have discovered the hysterical methods of these revolutionary humans…. In place of the United States Government we should have the horror and terrorism of Bolsheviki tyranny. Every scrap of radical literature demands the overthrow of our existing government.

A. Mitchell Palmer, 'The Case Against the Reds', 1920[2]

workers in *Pravda* on 22 August 1918 and the creation in 1919 of the Communist International (Comintern), aimed at spreading the revolution. The 'red threat' coincided with other social disturbances, including racial riots and a resurgence of the Ku Klux Klan, labour unrest with numerous strikes, and an outbreak of violent attacks. On 16 September 1920 an explosion at the headquarters of J. P. Morgan and Company on Wall Street killed thirty-eight people. The troubles of 1919–20 brought to a head the often brutal struggles between capital and labour that surfaced in America in the early 20th century and gave them a Communist tinge, even if most of the key outrages were committed by anarchists. Attorney General A. Mitchell Palmer launched a clampdown, making arrests and deporting many. These measures succeeded in removing radicalism almost entirely from American society.

The initial enthusiasm in the West for the Bolshevik support of workers' rights, which waned in the 1920s, was resurrected by the Great Depression (1929–33). As capitalism seemed on the point of collapse, the Communist alternative appeared extremely attractive. In January–August of 1931 there were 100,000 American emigration

Wreckage from the bombing of J. P. Morgan Bank, Wall Street, September 1920.

America and the World, 1919–39

America entered the First World War in 1917, helping to defeat the Germans by November 1918 and dominating the Paris Peace Conference of 1919, which produced the Versailles Treaty and launched the League of Nations as an international mechanism for promoting collective security. But the US Congress failed to ratify the settlement with Germany and the League. The public mood of non-involvement led to the election of three Republican presidents in succession – Warren Harding, Calvin Coolidge and Herbert Hoover – who kept US engagement in international politics at a minimum.

In 1933 the Democratic candidate, Franklin D. Roosevelt, became president in the depths of the Great Depression. This reinforced isolationist attitudes just when the international scene was growing dangerous with Japanese aggression in China, Italian moves against Ethiopia and Albania and, above all, German violation of Versailles and territorial expansion into Austria, Czechoslovakia and Poland. But if America avoided engagement in international politics, it was ever more deeply involved economically. US businesses increasingly sold abroad and established factories overseas, such as the Ford plant in England, at Dagenham in Essex. US finance underpinned the revival of Germany in the 1920s through the Dawes (1924) and Young (1929) Plans. But these were private business initiatives rather than government-led actions.

President Roosevelt waves to crowds in Rockport, Maine, on his return from meeting Winston Churchill, August 1941.

applications: for the first time in its history, more people wanted to leave than were entering the United States. Many were also attracted by Moscow's calls for a popular front of all left-wing groups against fascism. The Soviets seemed the only serious opponents of Mussolini's Italy and Hitler's Germany. They also backed the fight against Franco in the Spanish Civil War of 1936–39.

Adolf Hitler after giving a major speech, 1933.

The 1930s also saw a change in US government attitudes towards the Soviet Union. In 1920 the Americans had adopted a policy of non-recognition of Moscow. But when Franklin D. Roosevelt was elected as US president he recognized the Soviet Union in 1933, hoping to build better relations. Both countries had pressing internal priorities. Roosevelt became president in dire economic circumstances – there was 25 per cent unemployment – that compelled him to concentrate on domestic recovery. Stalin was preoccupied with his industrialization programme, pursued in a series of

OPPOSITE Photograph by Dorothea Lange of a Mexican migrant worker and child during the Great Depression, California, 1937.

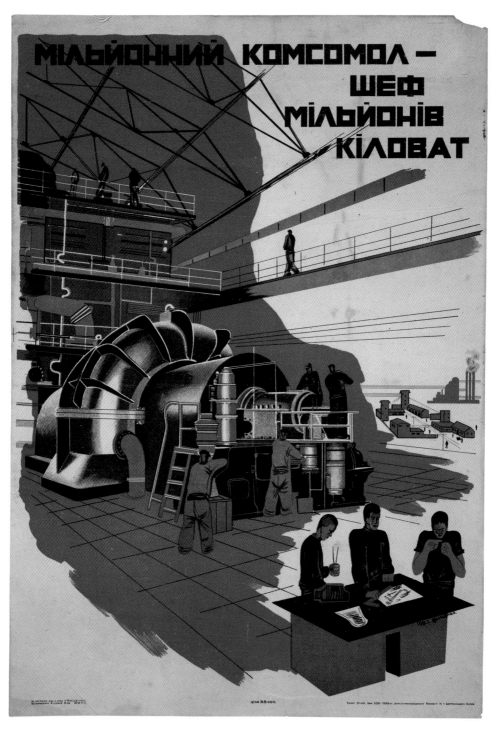

five-year plans. US-Soviet relations amounted to wary accommodation until almost the end of the decade. Some Americans were more sceptical of closer ties, particularly after the Soviets began major purges, especially against the military, in 1938–39. Others encouraged cooperation, and none more than Joseph Davies, ambassador to Moscow 1936–38.

German troops parade through Warsaw, September 1939.

Roosevelt's growing concern about Nazi Germany should have brought US-Soviet cooperation, especially after the German attack on Poland in September 1939. But a secret Nazi-Soviet deal allowed Moscow to occupy eastern Poland and the Baltic states. In November the Soviets attacked Finland. This confirmed for many the cynical nature of a leadership whose vicious qualities were made evident in the show trials, imprisonments and widespread executions of the late 1930s. When the American Communist Party supported the Nazi-Soviet Pact, the Roosevelt administration imprisoned its leader, Earl Browder, for passport fraud. In addition, the Americans introduced tough regulations on affiliation to foreign organizations, forcing the party in 1940 to end its formal membership of the Comintern.

The increasing gravity of the war has led me to feel that the principles of the Atlantic Charter ought not to be construed so as to deny Russia the frontiers she occupied when Germany attacked her.

Winston Churchill to Franklin D. Roosevelt, 7 March 1942[3]

The German invasion of the Soviet Union in June 1941 ended Washington's coolness to Moscow. Both the Americans (after some initial hesitation) and the British now backed the Soviet Union. Soon American Lend-Lease aid was arriving – totalling about $10 billion by the end of the war. The fundamental differences between American liberal democracy and free enterprise, on one side, and the Soviet planned economy and restricted freedoms, on the other, were forgotten. Newspapers and magazines extolled the virtues of the Soviet fight against the Nazis. Hollywood produced films about their heroic resistance, such as *North Star* (1943), starring Dana Andrews and Anne Baxter, and *Days of Glory* (1944), starring Gregory Peck. The outlook of Joseph Davies was once more in vogue. He published an account of his ambassadorship, *Mission to Moscow* (1941), which in 1943 was made into a film directed by Michael Curtiz, who had directed *Casablanca* the year before.

ABOVE Poster for the film *Mission to Moscow* (1943).

Hołd pruski w Moskwie

STALIN. – Pakt my tobie, Ribbentropie podpisali. Ty w rączkę nas pocaluj, pakt bierz, a co my zrobimy dalej, to jeszcze podumajem.

Polish cartoon satirizing the Molotov-Ribbentrop Nazi-Soviet Pact, August 1939.

Historic meeting of Soviet and American soldiers near Torgau, Germany, April 1945.

The wartime alliance of Britain, the Soviet Union and the United States continued until the defeat of Germany in May 1945. The British and Americans were willing to make concessions to the Soviets, and both Roosevelt and Winston Churchill, the British prime minister (1940–45), accepted Soviet territorial gains since 1939. But despite Anglo-American pliability, the alliance experienced frequent difficulties. Moscow complained about the tardiness and scale of Lend-Lease aid as well as delays in launching a 'second front', a cross-channel invasion of France. Poland posed particular difficulties, yet Roosevelt downplayed the discovery of Polish mass graves at Katyn and the Soviet failure to assist the August 1944 Warsaw Uprising.

Churchill was wary of the spread of Soviet power and Roosevelt's indifference to this trend. He met Stalin in Moscow in October 1944 and reached a deal on their separate spheres of influence: Greece would be 90 per cent British, Romania 90 per cent Soviet, Bulgaria 75 per cent Soviet, and Hungary and Yugoslavia

The Warsaw Ghetto, destroyed by German forces, 1945.

The division of Berlin into sectors, depicted in a map of 1961.

50 per cent each. The Americans officially opposed such spheres, so Roosevelt would not formally endorse the deal, though he appeared unconcerned by it.

When the Big Three met at the Yalta conference in February 1945 the atmosphere was cordial. In the face of increasing anxieties about Soviet actions in Eastern Europe, Roosevelt and Churchill persuaded Stalin to adopt the Declaration on Poland, which promised a broadening of representation in the Warsaw government and free elections. The Declaration on Liberated Europe committed the occupying powers to hold free and unsupervised elections in their zones at the earliest possible time. Germany would be divided into British, Soviet, American and French zones of occupation; the capital, Berlin, which was situated within the Soviet zone, would have American, British, French and Soviet sectors. German division would not be permanent and they would aim to treat Germany as a single economic unit. So the conference ended on a positive note. Indeed, Roosevelt encouraged an overly optimistic outlook.

Roosevelt died on 12 April and was succeeded by Harry Truman, who adopted a more direct style and was quicker to respond to problems than his predecessor. However, he was anxious to continue what he believed were Roosevelt's policies. He accused the Soviet foreign minister, Vyacheslav Molotov, of not honouring the Yalta agreements. Molotov responded, 'I have never been talked to like that in my life.' Truman's blunt riposte was: 'Carry out your agreements and you won't get talked to like that.'[4] But for all his tough talk, Truman accepted Averell Harriman's belief that a US-Soviet working relationship could be maintained. As a result, the next meeting of the wartime allies at Potsdam in July–August 1945 produced various agreements. The occupying powers would be permitted to collect reparations from their zones, and the Soviets could make additional collections from Western zones. Britain and the United States accepted the Oder-Neisse German-Polish border. The Soviets also confirmed their readiness to enter the fight against Japan. However, the Pacific war came to a swift end after the Americans dropped atomic bombs on Hiroshima and Nagasaki on 6 and 9 August.

Churchill, Truman and Stalin at the Potsdam conference, 2 August 1945.

Crowd celebrating
VE Day in New York City,
8 May 1945.

When the war ended in 1945 the prospects for future cooperation were mixed. The popular joy that greeted the end of hostilities
translated into a continuation of wartime feelings of amity towards
the Soviet Union. There was also a clear movement to the left in
European politics: the Labour Party came to power in Britain and
large Communist parties emerged in Italy and France. Moreover, the
wartime experience seemed to endorse the socialist notions of planning and government intervention. On the other hand, the temporary common cause had disappeared and the intrinsic differences
seemed likely to resurface. Yet throughout 1945 attempts were made,
even by Truman, to continue collaboration. Ideological disagreements after the Second World War mattered far more than after the
First World War, because this time both the Soviets and the Americans had substantial power and were in contact with each other, particularly in Germany. Their differences would now amount to more
than arguments over competing visions of economics and politics:
ideological disputes were bolstered by geopolitical ones. Would the
United States enter a contest with the Soviets over Europe or withdraw as they had done in 1920?

Chapter 2

Confrontation: 1945–1950

On 2 September 1945 the Second World War finally ended with the formal surrender of the Japanese on board the USS *Missouri*. The wartime allies had to begin the tasks of postwar adjustment and cooperation in the face of the immense human and physical costs of the conflict. Total deaths reached nearly 60 million. Soviet fatalities may have been 25 million, about 14 per cent of the prewar population. The country lost 6 million buildings and 25 million were left homeless. Britain's 400,000 deaths and America's 300,000 deaths (0.7 and 0.2 per cent respectively of their prewar populations) were small by comparison. Britain lost approximately a quarter of its national wealth and had to seek a loan of $3.75 billion from Washington. The Soviet Union managed to rebuild its heavy industries in the next decade, but agricultural production in 1952 was still below the figures for 1940. On the other hand, the United States economy saw a vast expansion – GNP rose from $886 million in 1939 to $118 billion in 1945. The dominance of American economic and military power was magnified, temporarily, by the losses of the other countries, but it inevitably made the United States confident about achieving its postwar goals. Even so, the Americans also experienced adjustment problems. Initial fears of a postwar slump gave way to concerns about inflation, as the pent-up demand for goods was released.

The euphoria of Victory in Europe (VE) Day had long dissipated but popular sentiment was still optimistic, despite the war's gruesome toll. Cities were devastated, especially in Germany and Japan; there were millions of refugees and displaced people; local and

The formal Japanese surrender on USS *Missouri*, Tokyo Bay, 2 September 1945.

OPPOSITE Czechoslovak Communist poster depicting a Soviet soldier reproving an American soldier, who leans back on a bomb labelled 'monopolistic capitalism'.

American automobile manufacture: Lincoln Continentals in Dearborn, Michigan, 1946.

national governments had collapsed, and certain countries (such as Greece, Yugoslavia and Korea) saw fierce struggles for political control. But populations across Europe were hopeful that they had at least taken the first step towards brighter times, while Americans felt the future was promising. After the basic rudiments of political life were re-established, left-wing parties enjoyed a surge of popularity as voters sought a better future. In Britain the Labour Party won the 1945 general election, while in France and Italy Communist parties challenged the Social Democrats for leadership of the socialist cause in their national assemblies.

It was in this context that the British, American and Soviet governments evinced a desire to continue their wartime cooperation. September 1945 saw the first meeting of the wartime allies in the forum agreed at Potsdam – the Council of Foreign Ministers (CFM). The London CFM (September–October), however, proved disappointing. Molotov wanted a say in the occupation regimes for Italy and Japan and repeated the demand, raised at Potsdam, that the Montreux Convention of 1936, an international agreement that restricted the movement of non-Turkish shipping through the

OPPOSITE Queuing for rations in Hamburg, March 1946.

Dardanelles and Bosphorus, be abolished and replaced by a new Soviet-Turkish arrangement. The Soviets insisted that the regimes they had installed in Bulgaria and Romania be recognized, which Britain and the US declined to do. In turn, the Soviets refused to allow China and France to be involved in making the peace treaties, saying only the three wartime allies should frame them. No progress was made about Germany's future, and the meeting ended in intemperate exchanges.

Yet the Americans did not abandon their quest for cooperation. James Byrnes, Secretary of State since July, continued to seek a compromise. Without consulting the British, he suggested to Molotov that another CFM be held in Moscow. The Soviets accepted the proposal, as did the British foreign secretary, Ernest Bevin, despite his resentment at Byrnes's clear attempt to bypass him. The Moscow CFM in December satisfied Byrnes's expectations. The Soviets accepted an American scheme for international control of atomic energy, but the detailed plan in 1946 contained an inspection regime unacceptable to Moscow. While the Americans gave the Soviets a small role in the occupation administration in Japan, arrangements

NO MORE DOLE QUEUES....SO IT'S

LABOUR

FOR SECURITY

VOTE LABOUR FOR SELF-RESPECTING JOBS

Labour Party poster for the British General Election, July 1945.

ABOVE US Secretary of State James Byrnes signs British Loan Agreement, 6 December 1945, with Under Secretary Dean Acheson standing (centre) behind him.

were made to widen political representation in the Bulgarian and Hungarian governments. Byrnes could now claim that the regimes deserved American diplomatic recognition and so could participate in the making of peace treaties.

These agreements produced a temporary improvement in US-Soviet relations. But Byrnes's efforts came under increasing domestic criticism for making too many concessions to Moscow. His critics deliberately talked of 'appeasement', with all its pejorative connotations. In addition, his tendency to assume he knew the best course for policy and his failure to consult the president adequately led to difficulties with Truman. Pressure to be tougher towards Moscow came not only from the president, Congress and the public. On 9 February 1946 Stalin spoke in an election address of the inescapable conflict between Communists and capitalists, and the speech disturbed various critics of the Soviets. The Under Secretary of State, Dean Acheson, was persuaded to ask George F. Kennan, then chargé d'affaires at the US embassy in Moscow, to evaluate Soviet policy. The result was the famous 'Long Telegram' of 22 February that argued for a tougher attitude to Soviet expansionism: Moscow should face, in the words of an article Kennan would write anonymously in 1947, a 'policy of containment'.[1] This undoubtedly influenced Byrnes to harden his outlook.

In the following month Winston Churchill, now out of office, delivered a speech in Fulton, Missouri, that has become emblematic of the emergence of a Cold War. He declared that an 'iron curtain'

Winston Churchill delivering his 'Iron Curtain' speech, 5 March 1946.

had descended on Europe 'from Stettin in the Baltic to Trieste in the Adriatic'.[2] Although he was accompanied by Truman, Churchill's words were not as influential as they seem in retrospect. The president already shared his perspective, but the American people were a little cool, particularly about his call for a renewed Anglo-American partnership to combat the new threats.

An opportunity to test the new more robust American attitude came in a crisis over Iran. During the war Britain and the Soviet Union had jointly occupied Iran to prevent its pro-Axis government from giving the Germans access to its oil. The Americans had also placed some troops in the country to oversee Lend-Lease aid to the Soviets. The London CFM agreed that the Allied forces would leave Iran six months after the end of war with Japan – meaning a deadline of 2 March 1946. The Soviets promised to negotiate, but then demanded an oil concession and supported separatists in Azerbaijan. The Americans adopted a tough response, no doubt influenced by Iran's position as the fourth largest producer of crude petroleum. When the deadline passed, they accused Moscow of breaking its commitment to the territorial integrity of Iran. Washington's anxieties rose with reports of Soviet troop movements and intelligence that the Soviets might coerce the Iranians into accepting a Moscow-friendly government. But then the Soviets announced their intention to remove their forces. The US felt its pressure had worked. In fact,

OPPOSITE Joseph Stalin's election address, Moscow, 9 February 1946.

US Lend-Lease planes,
Abadan, Iran.

it had only given a stronger hand to the skilful negotiations of the Iranian prime minister, Ahmad Qavam, who promised Moscow control of a joint oil company if the forces were removed. After the Soviet troops had departed, however, he sent Iranian forces to put down the separatists, and the Iranian parliament cancelled the oil deal.

Byrnes made a further effort to negotiate with the Soviets in the spring and summer of 1946 at the Paris CFM. He presented a proposal for a twenty-five-year treaty between the four main powers that would demilitarize Germany. Soviet insistence that they settle reparations first ended any prospect of agreeing on the treaty. Stalin expected American forces would leave and that he would be able to weaken the British and thereby secure a united but Soviet-friendly Germany. The CFM, sitting as a peace conference in a series of sessions until November, did manage, however, to produce peace treaties with Bulgaria, Romania, Hungary, Italy and Finland.

The failure of progress on Germany brought to the fore the daily troubles of administering the separate zones and of cooperation between the different zonal authorities. Inability to move forward on economic unity led the Americans and British, in July, to agree to the economic merger of their occupation zones – the Bizone, which came into effect in January 1947, ended the Potsdam commitment to treat

US Army map of occupation zones of Germany, 1945.

Germany as a single economic unit. The British took the lead in urging this, for the costs of their zone were becoming burdensome. In July 1946 they had introduced bread rationing, which they had avoided during the war. Byrnes announced the new approach in a widely publicized speech in Stuttgart in September. The United States would rebuild the Western-controlled zones of Germany whether

British military police erecting a sign marking the division between British and Soviet sectors in Berlin, 1948.

or not the Soviets agreed. He said, 'The German people throughout Germany, under proper safeguards, should now be given the primary responsibility for the running of their own affairs.... The United States favors the early establishment of a provisional Government for Germany'. Byrnes ended this major speech by implicitly warning the Soviet Union: 'We do not want Germany to become a satellite of any power. Therefore, as long as there is an occupation army in Germany, American armed forces will be part of that occupation.'[3] They would certainly stay beyond the eighteen months envisaged in 1945.

As cooperation proved increasingly difficult over Germany, a war scare arose over Turkey. Having been persuaded of the Soviet threat, Acheson felt the Soviets were trying to make Turkey a satellite. He persuaded the president to demonstrate American determination by sending a naval task force to Istanbul. In October the Soviets eased their pressure on Ankara, and once again Washington concluded that a firm response had yielded dividends.

The more decisive George C. Marshall replaced Byrnes in January 1947. After attending the Moscow CFM of March–April, he concluded that the Soviets did not want to reach agreements on key questions and on Germany especially. In the next few months he oversaw significant new initiatives. The first was in the eastern Mediterranean. On 21 February the British said they could no

USS *Missouri* and other American vessels off Istanbul, April 1946.

longer afford to aid the royalists in the Greek civil war or provide financial aid to Turkey. Acheson persuaded Marshall and Truman that the US should replace the British commitment, lest Greece and Turkey fall under Soviet influence or control. On 12 March Truman spoke to a joint session of Congress and enunciated what became known as the Truman Doctrine, offering help to nations deemed to be in danger of internal or external subjugation. He sought $400 million in aid to Greece and Turkey. The speech, and the testimony of Marshall and Acheson, spoke in apocalyptic terms of a global threat. Although the Soviet Union was not specifically mentioned, it was abundantly clear to all that it was the focus of the administration's anxieties. Congress accepted Truman's request and the president signed it into law on 22 May. For all its universalist vocabulary, the Truman Doctrine was not the blueprint for global containment that Acheson's later critics claimed.

The Truman administration also set about reorganizing the machinery of government so that it could respond more effectively to threats. The National Security Act of July 1947 created a number of new institutions: the Department of Defense, gathering the armed forces into one agency; the Central Intelligence Agency (CIA); and the National Security Council (NSC), a smaller, more specialized forum than the Cabinet in which to discuss major security issues.

Concern about failure to make progress on Germany and the likely damage to Europe's economy led Marshall to say on 28 April: 'The patient is sinking while the doctors deliberate.' On 5 June 1947 he launched an offer to extend US economic assistance to Europe. Unlike the Truman Doctrine, this time the appeal was more humanitarian than geopolitical. 'Our policy is directed not against any country or doctrine but against hunger, poverty, desperation and chaos'.[4] He urged the Europeans to draft a joint plan for recovery that the US could support. Both Czechoslovakia and Poland expressed an interest in attending the initial Paris meeting for what would become popularly known as the Marshall Plan. During trade talks with the Czechs, Stalin condemned Marshall's initiative as a device to isolate the Soviet Union; Poland and Czechoslovakia decided not to send representatives to Paris. The Western Europeans quickly responded, formulating a detailed scheme by September. The European Recovery Program (ERP) brought nearly $13 billion to help

Inter-europäische Zusammenarbeit
für bessere Lebensbedingungen

TOP George C. Marshall.

ABOVE Poster by Alfred Lutz promoting the Marshall Plan, 1950.

various Western European countries between 1948 and 1952. Contemporaries regarded the ERP as absolutely vital to economic recovery, although more recent writers have suggested its primary value lay in the impetus it provided for better economic reorganization and in the psychological boost it offered to European economic confidence. The Marshall Plan, for all its humanitarian motives, marked the Cold War division of Europe in economic terms, for in September 1947 the Soviets devised their own system of economic coordination within their sphere – the Communist Information Bureau (Cominform).

By 1948 fully fledged Cold War policies had emerged. The collapse of the London CFM of December 1947 and, even more, the seizure of power by the Communists in Czechoslovakia in spring 1948 hastened this development. Truman spoke to Congress on 17 March, saying the Communist takeover was 'a shock throughout the civilized world', and that it symbolized the 'increasing threat to governments who grant freedoms to their citizens'. He requested the reintroduction of selective national service and a programme of

universal military training lasting one year, aimed at producing a sizeable reserve force.[5] The Selective Service Act was signed into law on 24 June 1948.

Meanwhile, in June 1948 a major crisis developed in Berlin. By then the American, British and French sectors were increasingly regarded as a single entity, and in June these three powers introduced a reformed currency into West Berlin. The Soviets saw this as a challenge to the economic security of their sector and so imposed a blockade on all movement by train, road and waterway into the Western sectors of the city. Neither President Truman nor Marshall would back down in the face of this pressure. They decided on an airlift to provide supplies for the 2.5 million people in West Berlin, while rejecting any idea of using force to reopen routes to the city. The British and French supported this approach.

[I]n spite of General Clay's assurances, one couldn't close one's mind to the plain fact that, from the military point of view, Berlin's situation was hopeless...members of the Municipal Council were assaulted...cases of kidnapping and arbitrary arrests increased from month to month.

Willy Brandt, on the Berlin blockade of 1948–49[6]

The blockade, just like the treatment of Czechoslovakia over the ERP, indicated Stalin's determination to strengthen his control of the Soviet bloc. But he failed to impose his will on Yugoslavia, whose Communist Party remained loyal to their leader, Tito, and his independent line. In 1948 Tito broke with the Soviet Union and even secured some financial aid from the United States.

The Berlin crisis confirmed growing concerns among Western Europeans about their military vulnerability, and they sought some form of security guarantee. At the urging of the British, secret talks were held at the Pentagon in March 1948 on the possibility of a treaty or other guarantee of Western European security. In July 1948 formal talks on a North Atlantic Pact began in Washington with six other powers – Britain, Canada, France and Benelux. The North Atlantic

Berlin: Cold War Emblem

Berlin in 1945 symbolized victory over Nazi Germany. Divided into British, French, US and Soviet sectors and situated within Soviet-controlled East Germany, it witnessed the first major Cold War confrontation in the Soviet blockade of 1948–49. With the creation of the West German state, West Berlin became a Cold War

battleground, and this reached a peak in 1958–60. Moscow's threats owed a great deal to their fears for the survival of East Germany, whose population declined as many of its younger citizens left for the West through West Berlin.

The building of the Berlin Wall in 1961 solved the immediate problem

of migration from the East. The Cuban missile crisis of 1962 (see pp. 61–62) temporarily revived the risk of Soviet action there, but its resolution stabilized the situation. The city now seemed to be a vivid demonstration of the differences between the dismal, oppressive East and the richer, more vibrant and free West. However, West Berlin's youth exercised its freedoms in ways its authorities did not welcome – protesting against the government, the division of Germany, the Cold War and especially the Vietnam War. In November 1989 the opening and dismantling of the Berlin Wall was universally regarded as symbolic of the end of the Cold War.

The Berlin Wall under construction, 1961.

Treaty was signed by twelve powers in Washington on 4 April 1949. In May the Soviets lifted their blockade of Berlin, recognizing its failure. In the following months, the final details were settled for a West German constitution, whose main features had been agreed by Britain, Benelux, France and the United States in June 1948. The first government was elected in September 1949.

The self-confidence these achievements bred in Western leaders soon dissolved, especially in the United States. In September the Americans discovered that the Soviets had successfully exploded an atomic bomb in August – a particular shock since the CIA had advised Truman only in July that the Soviets were two years away from a bomb. In October Mao Zedong's Communists were victorious in China. The Republicans severely criticized the Truman administration for failing to prevent the 'loss' of China, regarded by many Americans as a special protégé. The feeling grew that Communism was now a greater danger and the Truman administration was not doing enough to combat it. Revelations of Soviet espionage added to the atmosphere of fear. Claims were made that these spies had greatly aided the Soviet atomic bomb project. Meanwhile,

BELOW Chairman Mao proclaims the founding of the People's Republic of China on the Tiananmen Gate rostrum, Beijing, 1 October 1949.

Propaganda Wars

The Cold War was a contest between two visions of the world as much as it was an episode in geopolitical rivalry. Governments ran propaganda campaigns to justify their policies on issues ranging from Germany to Korea to the Middle East. They deployed a huge range of methods: official speeches and press conferences, newspaper articles, pamphlets, newsreels, radio and television and motion pictures. The Soviets spoke of American imperialism in Asia and Latin America, economic rapacity across the globe, and consumerism. The US focused on the tyranny and lack of freedom in the Communist world and the merits of liberal democracy and market economies.

The battle for hearts and minds also became a cultural contest — in art, literature, music, theatre, dance and cinema as well as science, chess

scapegoats were identified within the United States. Communist sympathizers in government were accused of undermining support for Chiang Kai-shek's Chinese Nationalists. Senator Joseph McCarthy (Republican from Wisconsin) declared in February 1950 that the State Department was harbouring 205 Communists.

Early 1950 found the Truman administration under considerable pressure to demonstrate its firm resolve to prevent the spread of Communism in Asia. In February the Americans decided to develop

Step by step the Soviet writers uncovered the pernicious activities and dastardly methods of the cosmopolitan [read Jewish] doubledealers and their lickspittles. Like worms the anti-patriots gnawed at the healthy organism of our literature and art.

Pravda, 26 February 1949, on the Soviet literary scene in the 1940s[7]

and sport. Both the Soviets and the Americans aimed to demonstrate the superior culture of their own political system. Moscow championed classical music and artistic realism, while Washington promoted the modernism of jazz and abstract art, not least because of its repression in Communist countries. The Americans can be said to have won the propaganda wars, as the peoples of the Soviet bloc eventually rejected Communist politics and economics and embraced American popular culture – which US propagandists had done little to promote.

ABOVE *Poster issued in 1956 by the Information division of the US Army:* 'An American's Loyalty...Stronger Than Communist Treason!'

OPPOSITE *Cover of* Krokodil *magazine, 1951, depicting the UN as an instrument of Truman's aggressive policies in the Korean War.*

RIGHT *Krokodil cartoon of 1950, showing the US reaching out from the White House to control Korea, Iran, Turkey, Taiwan and Vietnam.*

the 'super', as the hydrogen bomb was then known. In February and March Acheson delivered tough speeches about the need to build 'situations of strength'. In May Washington extended military aid to the French in Indochina. Truman approved an evaluation of US military policy in the light of the loss of the nuclear monopoly. In response, Paul Nitze drafted NSC-68, which recommended a major programme of military expenditure to ensure America's ability to resist the Communist threat. This was enthusiastically endorsed by Acheson but Truman, dedicated throughout his presidency to budget restraint, decided not to act on recommendations that would require such a vast increase in defence spending. The robustness of the Truman administration's commitment to resisting Communism was about to be tested by the North Korean attack on South Korea.

Chapter 3

Crises and Neuroses: 1950–1962

In early 1950 the American government faced considerable domestic pressure to demonstrate its anti-Communist credentials. Republican critics blamed President Truman and Secretary of State Acheson for allowing the victory of the Communists in mainland China, urging them to support the Nationalists who had fled to the island of Taiwan (then called Formosa by Westerners). In addition, they faced accusations about Communist infiltration of government. It was in these circumstances that the Cold War turned into a hot war – on 25 June 1950 the Soviet-aided North Koreans attacked American-backed South Korea.

Korea had emerged in 1945 as an Asian version of Germany. Under Japanese control since 1910, it was divided into two occupation zones at the 38th parallel. Soviet forces occupied the North, while American troops entered the South. Soon separate governments were formed, despite a commitment to a united country with a single government. Both Kim Il-sung's Communist regime in the North and Syngman Rhee's authoritarian administration in the South claimed they were the rightful government of the whole peninsula. All American forces left the South by July 1949, but Washington continued to offer economic and military assistance sufficient to deter the North but not enough to encourage action by the South. Soviet forces withdrew in December 1948 but military advisers remained, and Moscow provided weapons, in particular T-34 tanks, which made North Korea more powerful than its southern neighbour.

OPPOSITE Kim Il-sung in a North Korean propaganda poster.

Kim made repeated requests to Moscow to be allowed to attack and conquer the South. In January 1950 Stalin eventually gave his approval. The risks, he calculated, were more likely to fall on the Chinese, which suited his wish to see them entangled with the US. Some historians feel that Acheson's 12 January speech, saying that South Korea remained outside the US defensive perimeter and so could not expect automatic military assistance, led Stalin to discount an American military response. This might have encouraged Stalin to think the risks were worth taking, but he warned Kim in March–April meetings that Soviet forces would not help, even if the Americans intervened.

The Americans felt bound to act against the attack, if they were to prove they were serious about resisting the spread of Communism. They sponsored United Nations resolutions condemning the aggression and urging UN members to offer forces to help the South Koreans. The United States led a UN force, under General Douglas A. MacArthur, which faced real difficulties in July and August before it repelled the invaders, driving them back across the 38th parallel border and further north to the frontier with China by late October. Chinese forces then intervened and threatened the Americans with defeat in December 1950–January 1951. There were real fears that the war might extend to China and its ally the Soviet Union, and that it might go nuclear. Truman pursued a limited war, despite

The first UN troops to cross the 38th parallel hold a sign marking the move.

US air strike on rail tracks, Wonsan, North Korea, 1950.

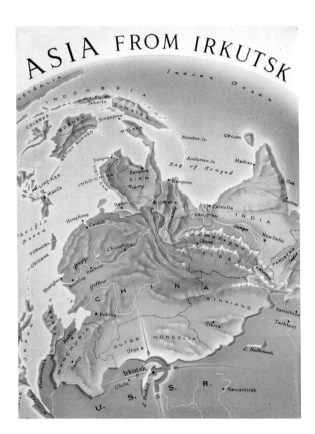

Time magazine map of 1952, visualizing Asia from the Soviet perspective.

MacArthur's pressure to act against China. The front was stabilized by early summer 1951, thanks to the effective generalship of Matthew B. Ridgway as commander on the ground and then as supreme commander when he replaced MacArthur, who was dismissed after publicly criticizing the president's strategy. For the next two years there was a bloody stalemate – up to three million Koreans were killed, wounded or missing and 33,651 Americans were killed – until President Eisenhower managed to achieve an armistice in July 1953.

The Korean War militarized the Cold War: US defence expenditure rose from 33 per cent of the budget in 1950 to 60 per cent of the budget in 1953, when it amounted to $53 billion. It also provoked a major programme of rearmament by all the Western powers, including a decision to allow German rearmament. By 1955 West Germany was a member of NATO and the Soviets had created the

ТРУЖЕНИЦЫ КИТАЯ в БОРЬБЕ за СОВЕТСКУЮ ВЛАСТЬ

ПРОТИВ ГОМИНДАНА И ИМПЕРИАЛИСТОВ ИДУТ в ПЕРВЫХ РЯДАХ

Until the 1960s the Soviet Union and Communism were treated as synonymous by the press and public and by many in government in the West. This is hardly surprising since, for over thirty years after 1917, the Soviet Union was the only Communist state. In addition, the Soviet liberation of Eastern Europe in 1944–45 led to the imposition of Communist regimes in these countries. When Mao Zedong's Communists gained power in China in 1949, many expected the new rulers would fall under Soviet influence, an impression reinforced by Mao's long visit to Moscow resulting in a Sino-Soviet alliance in February 1950. This viewpoint appeared in numerous newspaper articles and cartoons. A map in *The Washington Post* in 1950 treated Eastern Europe and China as part of the Soviet Union. However, many senior Americans and Europeans realized that, while East European regimes were subservient to Moscow, Sino-Soviet Union relations were less straightforward. The two countries disagreed on many issues including their long common frontier, which led to tensions and, in the 1960s, armed clashes. During Mao's Cultural Revolution in the mid 1960s the two nations competed for leadership of the international Communist movement, each charging the other with that most grievous of offences – 'revisionism'.

Soviet poster supporting the Chinese fight against the Japanese, 1932.

OPPOSITE ABOVE Senator Joseph McCarthy (right) alleging Communist infiltration of the US Army, 5 June 1954. The US Army's lawyer, Joseph Welch (with hand on head), famously said on 9 June: 'Have you no sense of shame, sir, at long last?'

Warsaw Pact with its East European satellites as a counter alliance. Korea also sharpened divisions in Asia. The US-Chinese rift deepened, as the Americans granted $125 million in military aid to Taiwan in 1950. The signature of the official Treaty of Peace with Japan in September 1951 was the prelude to improving US-Japanese relations, made easier by the boost to the Japanese economy from $2.3 billion of US procurements.

Korea intensified the burgeoning 'red panic' at home in the United States. In the late 1940s the House Un-American Activities Committee (HUAC) began investigating Communist influences in American society, deliberately seeking a higher profile by turning its attention to Hollywood. The investigations took an ugly form, particularly when they were reinforced by Senator McCarthy's anti-

Communist demagoguery. The frequent discovery of Western spies working for the Soviet Union added to the atmosphere of anxiety: Klaus Fuchs (1949–50), Guy Burgess and Donald Maclean (1951), and Ethel and Julius Rosenberg (tried in 1951 and executed in 1953). The paranoia about the Communist threat and the illiberal behaviour proved a boon to Soviet propaganda, but it also distorted domestic politics and damaged the lives of many American citizens.

BELOW Protesters against the atomic spies Julius and Ethel Rosenberg, 17 February 1953.

Red Channels (1950), a pamphlet listing 151 actors, writers, musicians, broadcast journalists and others, claiming they aided the Communist manipulation of the entertainment industry.

The attacks on individuals, the blacklisting of those denied work in the media and the general atmosphere of panic reached a peak in 1954–55. Although McCarthyite fears of Communist infiltration of American government and society gradually dissolved after the US Army successfully rebuffed the Senator's allegations, the quasi-religious fervour lingered. In the face of McCarthy's sustained attacks on the State Department, the Army and the presidency, there was a hardening of official opinion. In the United States this was an era of simplifications and stark East-West divisions, so Communists, socialists and even liberals were often lumped together as enemies of 'the American way of life'. The same panic and simplification did not take hold in Western Europe, where the security services worried about Communist infiltration but the people, many of whom voted for socialists, were less disturbed. Indeed, numerous blacklisted figures, such as the film director Joseph Losey and the actor Sam Wanamaker, were able to make successful careers in the British film industry.

The Communist threat began to appear in the cinema in the late 1940s: *The Woman on Pier 13* (1949) starred Robert Ryan as a former Communist seeking to thwart their latest conspiracy. In the 1950s McCarthyite neuroses found expression in movies; one of these, *Big Jim McLain* (1952), offered the improbable sight of John Wayne hunting Communists in Hawaii. The messages in these films were

RIGHT Herblock cartoon that coined the term 'McCarthyism' in 1950.

FAR RIGHT Poster for the movie *Big Jim McLain* (1952).

Anti-Communist magazine covers: the comic book *Is This Tomorrow?* (1947), *The American Legion Magazine* (1951) and the comic book *Atomic War!* (1952).

only a small part of a much wider trend of anti-Communism campaigns in America. Truman introduced various schemes designed to persuade the American public and US allies of the dangers of Communism. It was only with the Eisenhower administration, however, that a concerted programme was undertaken. The United States Information Agency (USIA), created in 1953, became a vital instrument for delivering America's propaganda messages worldwide.

US Strategic Air Command B-47 Stratojet bombers, the world's first swept-wing bomber.

Eisenhower's 'New Look' defence policy emphasized nuclear weapons as a deterrent against Soviet aggression. This reflected American nuclear superiority – in 1950 the Soviets had only a handful of weapons compared with the American stockpile of 369. But it was also a way of controlling the escalating costs of conventional forces. Despite the seemingly assertive nature of the new strategy, Eisenhower displayed restraint in Korea and also in Indochina,

[There is] what you would call the 'falling domino' principle. You have a row of dominoes set up, you knock over the first one, and what will happen to the last one is the certainty that it will go over very quickly. So you could have a beginning of a disintegration...the loss of Indochina, of Burma, of Thailand, of the Peninsula, and Indonesia.

President Eisenhower, press conference, 7 April 1954[1]

despite calls to commit US forces to aid the French. In 1954 French defeat was quickly followed by a settlement at Geneva, which established the independent states of Laos and Cambodia and temporarily divided Vietnam at the 17th parallel between a Communist north and a pro-Western south until all-Vietnam elections in 1956. Vietnam now became the focus of Cold War tensions. Eisenhower encouraged the South Vietnamese to boycott the 1956 elections and extended economic and military aid totalling over $1 billion between 1955 and 1961.

ABOVE President-elect Dwight D. Eisenhower visiting troops in Korea, December 1952.

LEFT French Foreign Legionnaire in the Red River Delta, near Hanoi, supported by a tank provided by the USA, c. 1954.

Nuclear Weapons Strategy

Nuclear weapons presented a fundamental paradox. They were immensely powerful but not very useful weapons, as territories conquered through their use would be contaminated by radiation. Moreover, a nuclear war would virtually obliterate the territories of the two sides. New strategies took some time to emerge, as politicians, officials, the military and intellectuals absorbed the changing context. Three main theories of nuclear deterrence emerged. The doctrine of 'massive retaliation' was enunciated by the Eisenhower administration in its 'New Look' defence policy in 1953. It was rooted in America's clear superiority in these weapons. By 1955 the Soviets had also adopted 'massive retaliation'. President Kennedy (1961–63) adopted 'flexible response', the staged escalation of weaponry only turning to all-out retaliation as a last resort. As the US and the Soviet Union reached nuclear parity, a new doctrine of 'mutual assured destruction' (MAD) was proclaimed.

In time, anxieties about escalation and fears of contamination from testing led to internationally agreed

Two views of Trinity, the first atomic explosion, at White Sands, New Mexico, 16 July 1945.

ABOVE *The fireball.*

BELOW *The crater.*

Eisenhower's approach to Vietnam characterized his attachment to indirect means of advancing US interests. In 1953 he approved a coup in Iran, fearing the Mossadeq regime was vulnerable to Communist takeover. In 1954 he sanctioned the overthrow of the Arbenz regime in Guatemala, whose redistribution of land – which included the seizure, with compensation, of lands held by the American firm, the United Fruit Company – seemed dangerously Communist. The coup in Iran made clear that American anxieties extended to the

restrictions. The Test Ban Treaty (1963) was signed by the United States, Britain and the Soviet Union. In the 1970s the Strategic Arms Limitation Talks (SALT) agreements froze Soviet and American missile totals and limited those with multiple warheads. The Strategic Arms Reduction Talks (START) agreement (1991) halved numbers by 1998.

US hydrogen bomb test, Nevada, 25 May 1953.

Middle East, where they created a regional version of NATO – the Baghdad Pact of Turkey, Iran, Iraq and Pakistan – but did not become members.

The Egyptian government of Gamal Abdel Nasser became a particular focus of US concerns, especially after it acquired Czech armaments. Washington feared the spread of Soviet influence, for the shipments seemed consistent with contemporaneous Soviet support for 'national liberation' movements around the world. The Ameri-

Egyptian leader Gamal
Abdel Nasser greets
cheering crowds,
22 July 1954.

cans and British withdrew promises to help finance the Aswan Dam. In response, Nasser nationalized the Suez Canal in July 1956. Angry at this action against a British asset, and determined to demonstrate his country's continued great power status, the British prime minister Anthony Eden colluded with the French and Israelis and, without consulting Washington, sent forces into Egypt in November, ostensibly to regain control of the canal but mainly to remove Nasser. Eisenhower and his Secretary of State, John Foster Dulles, deplored the Anglo-French resort to gunboat diplomacy. The president was particularly outraged that they had acted aggressively at the same time as the crisis over the Soviets sending troops into Hungary to suppress its uprising against Communist control. American diplomatic and financial pressure on Britain forced a humiliating climb-down.

Eisenhower now articulated a policy of engagement. In March 1957 he secured Congressional approval for $200 million in aid as well as the authority to initiate US military intervention in any Middle Eastern country threatened by aggression or subversion – the Eisenhower Doctrine. The Americans briefly intervened militarily in Lebanon in 1957 and in Jordan in 1958, and this appeared to ease the immediate problems in these two countries.

For all Dulles's talk about 'rollback' of Soviet control, the Americans did not act to prevent the Soviet action in Hungary, confining themselves to condemnations. American restraint was to some extent matched by a Soviet readiness, apparent since Stalin's death in March 1953, to try to lessen tensions. In May 1955 Nikita Khrushchev agreed to Allied evacuation from, and the neutralization of, Austria (under four-power occupation since 1945), and withdrew Soviet troops from occupied Finnish territory. He also attended a summit meeting with Eisenhower and the French and British prime ministers at Geneva in July 1955 which, despite the failure of arms control proposals, led to a significant (if temporary) improvement in East-West relations.

With the geopolitical struggle stable, the United States remained, in general, socially conservative. Economic progress and apparent social stability encouraged political complacency. No significant domestic legislation was approved by Congress between 1945 and the early 1960s, except for the Highway Act of 1956, which funded the construction of a nationwide interstate highway network.

The percentage of foreign-born in the population fell from 15.6 per cent in 1950 to 13.4 per cent in 1960, reinforcing patriotic and conformist attitudes. Hollywood movies reflected this outlook: women were frequently cast in supporting roles such as housewives – in contrast to the films of the late 1930s and 1940s that featured strong women characters played by formidable actresses including Bette Davies, Joan Crawford, Barbara Stanwyck and Rosalind Russell. This was also the baby boom era: between 1946 and 1964 there were 76.4 million births, comprising 40 per cent of the US population of 192 million. Underpinning this social conservatism was economic growth, as GNP (in constant 1958 dollars) rose from $355.3 billion in 1950 to $487.7 billion in 1960.

Soviet leader Nikita Krushchev at the UN, 22 September 1960.

Soviet tanks in Budapest to put down the Hungarian Uprising, 1956.

Western Europe also experienced growing prosperity: German real GNP growth was 7.8 per cent in the 1950s, while Italy saw 6.4 per cent, France and the Netherlands 4.5 per cent and Britain 2.6 per cent. In addition, the continental Europeans decided to institutionalize cooperation: West Germany, France, Italy and the three Benelux countries created the European Economic Community in 1957. The EEC boosted European trade by reducing tariffs, and by 1960 the EEC Six accounted for 22.9 per cent of world trade.

Although on the surface the 1950s were a time of social and political stability, below were deep stirrings. These years saw the emergence of a youth revolution, as the era of full employment meant that young people for the first time were able to command ever higher wages as employers competed for new workers. The new-

Fans of rock 'n' roll star Bill Haley await his arrival at Waterloo station, London, 5 February 1957.

found power and social prominence of the young coincided with a major development in popular music, as rock 'n' roll, with its huge appeal to youth, emerged from rhythm and blues. Here was a coalescence of economic, social and cultural developments. Their purchasing power allowed the young to pursue their enthusiasm for rock 'n' roll and to cultivate their distinctive tastes in music, clothes, cars and social life. Led by Elvis Presley, American popular music and culture proceeded to conquer the globe. The roots of rock 'n' roll lay in black music, which had been a minority interest among white Americans during the segregation era. But the continuing discriminatory treatment of the black population, especially in the South, now saw the emergence of civil rights activists such as Dr Martin Luther King Jr. They won a landmark victory in the Brown v. Board of Education judgment issued by the Supreme Court in 1954, which declared so-called 'separate but equal' education was unconstitutional. In Little Rock, Arkansas in 1957 federal troops enforced the rights of nine black students to attend an all-white local high school. Dramatic changes were also occurring on the international stage: by the close of the decade both the French and British empires were

US Airborne troops outside the school in Little Rock, Arkansas, 1957.

beginning to break up as they granted independence to their African colonies.

The late 1950s also saw a new energy in the Soviet Union. The last years of Stalin's rule were bitter, but his death in March 1953 and the emergence of Khrushchev by 1955 marked a new phase. Prisoners were released from the Gulag system of prison labour camps and secret police activities were reduced. The intelligentsia, based mainly in Moscow and Leningrad, felt able to test the limits of state censorship. They were further encouraged when Khrushchev made the 'secret speech' (so called because it was delivered to a closed session of selected party officials, although it was soon leaked) to the 20th Communist Party Congress on 25 February 1956 – a four-hour documentation of Stalin's personal responsibility for the purges. There was talk of a cultural thaw. Khrushchev approved publication of Alexander Solzhenitsyn's *One Day in the Life of Ivan Denisovich*, which released a flood of articles about the labour camps and the terror. Yet there were limits to the new toleration. Boris Pasternak's *Doctor Zhivago*, which brought him the 1958 Nobel Prize for Literature, was banned, and hundreds, perhaps thousands, of academics lost their posts in retaliation for radical criticism of the regime.

Whether you like it or not, history is on our side. We will bury you!

Nikita Khrushchev to Western ambassadors, Polish embassy, Moscow, 18 November 1956[2]

Khrushchev wanted to revitalize the economy, believing the Soviet Union could catch up with the West and surpass it. He sought to shift priorities from heavy industry to consumer goods in order to satisfy mounting domestic discontent, expand agricultural production and reduce the military's dominance of expenditure. He inspired the imagination of the young, leading over a million to volunteer to help cultivate 'virgin lands'. Official Soviet figures exaggerated

economic growth, but a recent study estimates rates of 5.2 per cent in the 1950s and 4.8 per cent in the 1960s. Millions of Soviet citizens moved from communal flats into self-contained apartments, and the increased privacy encouraged a growing freedom of speech. In addition, this era saw greater engagement of individual Russians with the outside (Western) world. The sale of short-wave radios increased dramatically as more people listened to foreign broadcasts; more American films became available; translated American literature appeared in Soviet libraries; and travel to and from the USSR was made easier. These laid the roots for a growing enthusiasm among

Apartments under construction in Moscow, 1964.

Soviet youth, from the 1960s onwards, for the new American music and clothes.

The seeming vitality of these early years of Khrushchev's rule led some to fear that the West was falling behind, both economically and technologically. In October 1957 the Soviets launched the first man-made satellite, Sputnik, while the first American attempt failed in December. There was talk of a 'missile gap' between the Soviet nuclear stockpile and the apparently inferior American supply. For many in the US, the stable and relaxed Eisenhower years now appeared dangerously complacent. This viewpoint was reinforced by Khrushchev's brinkmanship. The Soviet leader declared in November 1958 that, if the occupying powers did not agree on a settlement within six months, he would conclude a peace treaty with East Germany and put control of the access routes to West Berlin under East German supervision. Khrushchev then delayed his ultimatum, visited the United States, and agreed to discuss Berlin and other issues at a summit meeting in May 1960. However, the conference collapsed when the Soviets shot down and captured intact an American U-2 spy plane over their territory: Eisenhower rejected Khrushchev's demand for a full apology, after which the Soviet delegation walked out of the conference.

As the United States had become more militarized in its stance against Communism, senior military figures became adept at selling themselves to the public. Many movies in the 1950s credited the assistance of the US Department of Defense. Unsurprisingly, films such as *Strategic Air Command* (1955) projected a favourable image of the US armed forces. Yet the shrewd Eisenhower, a former general, warned in his valedictory address against the growth of the industrial-military complex, a grouping of defence businesses and military leaders who shared common goals and might push the country in a direction that would benefit them but not the people. John F. Kennedy assumed the American presidency in 1961 on a platform of a more dynamic approach to Berlin and other problems.

RIGHT Replica of Sputnik, the first artificial satellite, launched in October 1957.

BELOW Cartoon from *Krokodil* (1959), showing Sputnik over America.

For all his bluster, Khrushchev proceeded cautiously. On 12 August 1961 the East Germans constructed a wall separating East and West Berlin, thereby stemming the flow of refugees to the West. Kennedy did not react immediately. He sent a battle group of 1,500 men, who passed unhindered by Soviet and East German border guards. Content that Western access routes remained secure, the Americans accepted the new situation. They condemned the wall but saw that it removed Berlin as a pressing issue.

In the following year, however, there arose the greatest military confrontation of the Cold War. On 15 October 1962 American aerial reconnaissance uncovered a secret Soviet scheme to deploy nuclear missiles in Cuba. Khrushchev wanted to protect Cuba from American aggression. If Moscow was to be convincing as the leader of the

U-2 photograph of a Soviet truck convoy placing missiles near San Cristobal, Cuba, 15 October 1962: the first proof of their deployment.

ABOVE President Kennedy
signs the Proclamation for
the Interdiction of Delivery of
Offensive Weapons to Cuba,
23 October 1962.

Communist cause, then it had to demonstrate support for 'anti-imperialist' revolutions around the world, and Castro was very popular in the Soviet Union, especially among the educated young. In addition, Khrushchev saw this as an opportunity to improve the strategic balance at a time when the Americans were deploying Titan and Minuteman missiles that were superior to Soviet missiles.

The U-2 reconnaissance photographs, when analysed with the help of Oleg Penkovsky, a Soviet defector, revealed that missile sites were being constructed. Adlai Stevenson, US representative at the UN, favoured conciliation, suggesting a possible deal involving no Soviet nuclear weapons in Cuba and the removal of US Jupiter missiles in Turkey. Most American voices, especially the military, urged a much more vigorous response. Some demanded that they invade Cuba, others that they launch an air strike. President Kennedy adopted a tough but measured approach. He instituted a naval 'quarantine' of Cuba that aimed to stop Soviet ships from reaching the island. As Soviet vessels approached, tensions mounted, but then the ships turned back. In a letter of 26 October Khrushchev seemed ready for a deal, based on removal of the missiles in return for an end to the quarantine and an American promise not to invade Cuba. Yet the next day he demanded that the Americans must also remove their Jupiter missiles from Turkey. Publicly Kennedy refused to accept this, but through talks between his brother Robert F. Kennedy and the Soviet ambassador, Anatoly Dobrynin, he told the Soviets that once their missiles left Cuba, the Americans would quietly remove the Jupiter weapons. While this proposal was being communicated to Moscow, Khrushchev learned that a U-2 plane had been shot down over Cuba and that Kennedy intended to deliver an address to the nation. He wrongly believed that the president was about to announce the invasion of Cuba, so the Soviet leader accepted the terms of the RFK-Dobrynin deal. Both Kennedy and Khrushchev deserve credit for resisting the advice of hawks and finding a diplomatic solution, though clearly Khrushchev was avoiding the escalation of a situation largely of his own creation. Kennedy's handling of the crisis has been widely praised for his cool restraint. Yet some historians believe his vigorous anti-Castro measures had pushed Cuba towards the Soviets, and that a greater readiness to negotiate could have avoided confrontation.

American schoolchildren learn how to protect themselves in case of a nuclear attack by practising a duck and cover drill in their classroom, February 1951.

OPPOSITE BELOW Cuban leader Fidel Castro waves to cheering crowds in Havana after the flight of dictator Fulgencio Batista, 1 January 1959.

BELOW Poster for the movie *Dr Strangelove* (1964).

Cuba added to the concern growing from the late 1950s about atomic war, epitomized in Nevil Shute's novel *On the Beach* (1957), with its bleak picture of survivors of a nuclear attack awaiting death. The fear that trigger-happy military figures might provoke the outbreak of a nuclear war became pervasive and was captured in Stanley Kubrick's movie *Dr Strangelove* (1964). Yet for all the seriousness of the Cuban missile crisis and its exposure of the risks of nuclear escalation, the resolution of the crisis heralded a new and less dangerous era in US-Soviet relations.

Chapter 4

Cooperation and Protest: 1962–1972

The prospect of nuclear Armageddon, raised by the Cuban missile crisis, concentrated minds in both Washington and Moscow. Wishing to avoid misunderstanding in the future, they installed a telegraphic hotline between the Kremlin and the White House. In June 1963 President Kennedy publicly urged cooperation: 'Let us not be blind to our differences but let us also direct attention to our common interests and to the means by which those differences can be resolved.'[1] Yet there was some ambiguity in JFK's position: in that same month he took a tougher line during a visit to Berlin and soon revived the anti-Castro policy.

Kennedy's desire for engagement bore fruit in progress on a nuclear test ban. The growing fears about nuclear testing had produced US-Soviet-British talks in the late 1950s but they had reached deadlock on underground testing. The Cuban missile crisis spurred all the parties to find a solution. Renewed talks in Moscow between the United States, Britain and the Soviet Union led to the signature in August 1963 of a Partial or Limited Test Ban Treaty that banned testing in the atmosphere and under water – any future tests must take place underground. France refused to join, but by the late 1960s a hundred nations had agreed to adhere to it.

The urge to cooperate was not the only consequence of the October 1962 crisis. The Soviets recognized that America's overwhelming nuclear superiority had contributed to their climb-down, and Moscow now sought nuclear parity with the United States. In 1962 the United States had 203 intercontinental ballistic missiles

OPPOSITE President Kennedy's speech in front of Schoenberg Rathaus (City Hall), Berlin, 26 June 1963. He declared: 'Ich bin ein Berliner' (I am a Berliner).

Launch of US Air Force Atlas missile, 20 February 1958.

OPPOSITE ABOVE Military parade, Red Square, Moscow, 1969.

OPPOSITE BELOW Leonid Brezhnev.

BELOW President Lyndon B. Johnson.

(ICBMs), compared with the Soviet Union's 36. By the late 1960s the United States had 1,054 ICBMs and the Soviets possessed 1,140. NATO then adopted the concept of 'mutual assured destruction' (MAD). The Partial Test Ban Treaty was perhaps Kennedy's greatest accomplishment, but within three months he was dead, the victim of an assassin's bullet.

Vice-President Lyndon B. Johnson became president and went on to win the 1964 presidential election in a landslide. In little more than a year he initiated one of the great domestic reform programmes: a Civil Rights Act; federal aid for elementary and secondary education; Medicare to provide health insurance for the elderly and Medicaid to fund health benefits for low-income groups; immigration reform that removed previous discriminatory quotas; and the Voting Rights Act that eventually extended voting rights to black

Americans. Both Congress and public believed they could afford these measures. The American economy was booming – GNP rose from $487.7 billion in 1960 to $722.5 billion in 1970. Indeed, the West as a whole (especially West Germany, Japan and France) enjoyed a similar boom.

There was also a new leadership in the Soviet Union. In October 1964 Khrushchev was removed and replaced with Leonid Brezhnev as General Secretary of the Central Committee and Alexei Kosygin as Chairman of the Council of Ministers. The Central Committee no longer wanted one man to hold both posts. Kosygin was a technocrat, interested in pursuing efficiency and economic reforms within the existing system. He was progressively outmanoeuvred by the under-rated but more skilled political operator Brezhnev, who emerged in the 1970s as the dominant figure in the Kremlin.

The Second World War weakened the European empires in Asia. In the 1940s Britain granted independence to India, Pakistan, Ceylon and Burma; the Dutch East Indies became Indonesia; and by 1954 France had lost Indochina. By the late 1950s Britain and France had decided, in the face of financial pressures and the rising power of nationalism, to decolonize in Africa. A total of seventy-five new nations emerged after 1945, providing a potential new arena for Cold War competition.

Many leaders of the newly independent states, such as Nkrumah in Ghana and Sukarno in Indonesia, joined the non-aligned movement, founded at Bandung in 1955. But because many of the new African rulers adopted socialist policies, Washington feared that Soviet influence would now extend to these countries. However, few of these leaders wanted to replace colonial rule with dependence on another great power. In the 1970s US-Soviet tensions reached Africa. In 1975 the new revolutionary government in Portugal granted independence to Mozambique and Angola. Cuban troops were sent to help one of the factions in the Angolan civil war that followed, leading the Americans to back a rival group. The same happened in Namibia's struggle for independence from South Africa (1966–88).

Bandung Conference, 1955.

Both the Soviet pursuit of consolidation and Johnson's reform programme were disrupted by what became the dominant issue of the second half of the 1960s – Vietnam. Eisenhower had aided South Vietnam financially but had been wary of committing US forces, sending military advisers instead (totalling 685 in 1961). Kennedy greatly increased the number of advisers, so that by his death there were 16,732. This deeper involvement partly reflected changed circumstances. The threat to the southern regime had grown and required a response: in 1959–60 there were rural uprisings against Ngo Dinh Diem's government, and the southern Communists persuaded the North Vietnamese to help them.

But Kennedy was not merely reacting to circumstances. He viewed Vietnam in broader terms. By 1962–63 the European situation had stabilized and Cold War tensions spread to Asia, Africa and

Latin America, a process hastened by decolonization in the former British and French empires. Kennedy responded to Khrushchev's support for 'wars of national liberation' by promoting the idea of 'nation-building': the United States would help countries to improve their economies and establish political stability, and so avoid the spread of Communism. He also recognized that American voters would judge him partly on his defence of South Vietnam against Communism and, if he failed to do so, he risked not being re-elected.

Johnson was even more committed to resisting Communism. He accepted the 'domino theory', which maintained that a Communist victory in Vietnam would trigger Communist takeovers in other Asian countries. He immediately faced an escalation of the assault on the South; by 1964 the North Vietnamese army had begun operations in the South in support of the Vietcong (National Front for the Liberation of Vietnam, NLF). An incident in August 1964 provided an excuse to act against the North: US destroyers reported coming under attack by North Vietnamese torpedo boats in the Gulf of Tonkin.

US Marine with Vietcong suspect, 1965.

Despite uncertainty about the facts, Johnson adopted a tough response, keen to match the forceful anti-Communism of Barry Goldwater, his Republican opponent in the forthcoming presidential election. He ordered a retaliatory air strike and secured from Congress the so-called Gulf of Tonkin resolution, which authorized the president 'to repel any armed attack against the forces of the United States and to prevent further aggression'.[2] Johnson used this resolution (without a formal declaration of war) to justify subsequent bombing campaigns and the commitment of US ground forces against North Vietnam.

After his landslide victory in November 1964, Johnson was determined to act against the Vietcong. His Defense Secretary, Robert McNamara, reinforced this tough approach, saying they should act before the Vietcong destroyed the Saigon regime, whose forces were suffering a succession of defeats. Historians have debated whether, had he lived, Kennedy would have pursued the escalation of American involvement undertaken by LBJ. Certainly, Kennedy was more sceptical than Johnson about military advice, opposing requests for air strikes against the North. Yet America's global prestige was so entangled with support for the South that any abandonment of the regime would have been very difficult. Nevertheless, Johnson did not act immediately, for he wanted to secure passage of

OPPOSITE US bombing of North Vietnam, June 1966.

US helicopter spreading defoliant in the Mekong Delta, 1969.

his 'Great Society' legislation and feared that conservatives in Congress might support US involvement in Vietnam but claim that the social reforms would have to be restricted if the military costs were to be met. He told Congress in October 1966, 'We are a rich nation, and we can afford to make progress at home while meeting obligations abroad.'[3]

On 7 February 1965 the United States air base at Pleiku was attacked by the Vietcong. Johnson now agreed to a major bombing campaign against the North – 'Rolling Thunder'. The aim was to stabilize the military and political situation in South Vietnam and damage the North Vietnamese war effort. However, it failed – partly because the North lacked industrial targets and partly because of large-scale Soviet and Chinese aid to the North. As the military situation deteriorated in the South, Johnson agreed to send US ground forces, and their numbers steadily escalated. By 1968 there were 540,000, but the Americans failed to defeat North Vietnam and the Vietcong: they never succeeded in effectively halting the enemy's supplies of arms and men. However, the US commander General William Westmoreland remained convinced they were winning.

The rising American casualties (nearly 16,000 deaths by December 1967) led to growing discontent at home. In October 1967 a

ABOVE General Westmoreland (left) in Vietnam, 1966.

The guerrilla is the combat vanguard of the people...it will be a protracted war; it will have many fronts; and it will cost much blood and countless lives for a long period of time.

Che Guevara on guerrilla warfare, 1964[4]

demonstration at the Pentagon brought 30,000 protesters. Then, on 31 January 1968, the lunar New Year holiday of Tet, a sudden massive offensive by the North Vietnamese and the Vietcong shook public opinion in the United States. The offensive failed to overthrow the Saigon government or to instigate a popular uprising in the major cities, but it unsettled Congress as well as the people they represented. Television showed Marines fighting to keep control of the US embassy in Saigon. The fact that the Tet offensive could even be mounted, in the face of the Johnson administration's public optimism about the progress of the war, was a major blow to Johnson's credibility. The president's close advisers – 'the Wise Men', led by a new Secretary of Defense, Clark Clifford (McNamara, thinking the

war was unwinnable, resigned a month after the offensive began), and the former Secretary of State, Dean Acheson – told Johnson that victory was unlikely. Moreover, the economy was being severely damaged by the immense cost of the conflict, inflation was mounting and there were growing budget and balance of payments deficits. By 1968 the war's annual cost was $25.2 billion and there was a federal budget deficit of $24.2 billion.

Johnson refused Westmoreland's request for more troops; he also announced a partial ending of the bombing of Vietnam and declared that he would seek peace negotiations with the North Vietnamese. He also said he would not stand for re-election in November 1968. Peace talks began in Paris in spring 1968 but made no progress. North Vietnam and the Vietcong believed they had the Americans on the run and demanded the complete withdrawal of American forces and a change of government leading to the reunification of the country.

Cholon, South Vietnam, after the Tet offensive, 1968.

OPPOSITE BELOW Anti-Vietnam War poster: 'Bring the troops home now'.

The Tet crisis energized the opponents of US involvement in Vietnam throughout America and Western Europe. The worldwide protests of 1968 might have been triggered by events in Vietnam, but they had deeper roots. Those involved were principally the youth, who had become much larger both in numbers and as a proportion of the population. In the United States, those aged 15–24 rose from 24 million in 1960 to 35.3 million in 1970, 17.5 per cent of the population. A growing number of them went to university – in the US enrolments went up from 3.7 million in 1960 to 8.5 million in 1970, in West Germany from 203,000 to 386,000, in France from 216,000 to 602,000, and even in Britain they rose from 107,000 to 228,000. The prevailing ethos of progress affected the young and decision-makers alike. But young people were increasingly rejecting the institutions and attitudes of these decision-makers. Instead, activists were advocating the 'rights' of various groups, from blacks to Mexican-Americans, from homosexuals to women. The central assumptions of postwar Western societies were challenged not only by students but by a broad cross-section of ordinary citizens. Rapid economic growth had brought steadily improving material circumstances, which bred not complacent contentment but rising social and cultural expectations. Young people blamed their elders and their leaders for the limits on their lives. They criticized the Cold War mentality for obstructing social progress, although paradoxically US

Once they had broken the resistance of the guards, they entered the building, smashed the windows, destroyed the furniture, pulled down the portraits and destroyed them, beat up the functionaries of the Party, the Soviets and the KGB present at the location.

KGB report on the uprising of 2 June in Novocherkassk, 7 June 1962[5]

promotion of education (to compete with the Soviet Union) had done much to encourage this emerging counterculture. The combination of the war in Vietnam and this radical outlook generated a great deal of the protest in 1968.

The Soviet bloc was also touched by dissent. An early example came in June 1962 when workers occupied the Communist Party headquarters in Novocherkassk in protest at sharp increases in meat and butter prices. Military action resulted in the deaths of at least sixteen people. In the course of the 1960s the leadership became

1968: Year of Protest

Protest against authority grew in the 1960s and reached a peak in 1968. The University of California at Berkeley was in the vanguard with its Free Speech Movement of 1964–65, which forced the authorities to allow political protest by students. Students increasingly attacked US involvement in the Vietnam War, especially after the January 1968 Tet offensive. In April the assassination of the civil rights leader Martin Luther King triggered violence in 130 US cities. Meanwhile in Europe, protest demonstrations began in West Berlin and then spread to the rest of West Germany, Italy and, most memorably, France, where students in Paris were joined by industrial workers. The protests were mildest in Britain, which had fewer university students and a more reformist culture.

The Communist world was not immune. In the 'Prague spring', reformists in Czechoslovakia under Alexander Dubcek tried to pursue a more open policy until Brezhnev sent troops in to re-establish orthodoxy. In China Mao initiated the Cultural Revolution in 1966, setting the Red Guards on his opponents in the Communist Party. Such was the upheaval by late 1967 that the army in Wuhan turned on the Red Guards and, faced with the prospect of a civil war and loss of authority, Mao backed the military in 1968; he officially declared the Cultural Revolution over in 1969, although instability continued until 1976.

May Day protest, Paris, 1968, calling for the unconditional end to US bombing of North Vietnam.

increasingly concerned about the 'youth problem', as the young grew fond of Western pop music, opted out of the official youth organization (Konsomol) and voiced more critical comments. Many were also able to avoid military service. The majority of young people still supported official policies, but growing numbers were attracted to Western ways. As in the West, the young formed an increasing proportion of society – 70 million Soviets were born between 1945 and 1966. In Czechoslovakia a reformist party sought a different form of Communism, but they exceeded the limits of Moscow's tolerance of deviance from orthodoxy. The 'Prague spring' of 1968 ended when Soviet forces entered the country and removed the leaders.

The events in Vietnam in 1968 were an impetus for both the superpowers and the Europeans to explore better East-West relations, which came to be called détente. The French president Charles de Gaulle took the lead. He visited Moscow in June 1966 and hinted at recognizing the existence of two German states. West Germany also sought new openings with the East, establishing trade missions in Romania, Bulgaria, Poland and Hungary. Many West Europeans also wondered whether the preoccupation with Vietnam would undermine the American commitment to station ground troops in Western Europe and thus weaken NATO. From 1966 onwards the Democratic Senate Majority Leader Mike Mansfield sponsored Senate resolutions favouring substantial cuts in US forces in Europe.

As a result of de Gaulle's initiatives, NATO endorsed a relaxation of tensions. President Johnson now spoke of achieving 'peaceful engagement' with Eastern Europe. In June 1967 Johnson and Kosygin met in Glassboro, New Jersey and considered a possible treaty limiting their strategic nuclear weapons. The Johnson administration also

Prague residents wave Czechoslovak flags and surround Soviet tanks, part of the Soviet-led Warsaw Pact invasion to crush the 'Prague spring' reforms, 21 August 1968.

French President Charles de Gaulle in Moscow, June 1966.

BELOW NATO poster, 1970.

explored nuclear non-proliferation. In July 1968 the United States and the Soviet Union signed the Non-Proliferation Treaty. By 1985 some 131 countries had ratified it. In addition, they agreed to talks on Strategic Arms Limitation (SALT). Efforts were also made towards an anti-ABM (Anti-Ballistic Missile) treaty, but since Johnson was not seeking re-election, further progress would have to await the arrival of a new president.

The Soviet Union also looked more favourably on some kind of détente. This was in part a product of Brezhnev's personal inclinations: for all his commitment to a robust defence of orthodoxy, he eschewed Khrushchev's brinkmanship, hoping instead to be a peacemaker. In addition, its deteriorating relations with China worried Moscow, which feared Beijing's irrational belligerence. Perhaps, above all, their approximate nuclear parity with the Americans made the Soviets more comfortable that the talks would proceed on a basis of equality.

Richard Nixon won the November 1968 election. He appointed Henry Kissinger as his National Security Adviser, and they formed an unlikely partnership that dominated US foreign policy from 1969 to 1974 (Kissinger's influence continued under President Gerald Ford, 1974–77). William P. Rogers was appointed Secretary of State but he was largely sidelined, as Kissinger took the lead in developing policy proposals. In September 1973 Kissinger succeeded Rogers as Secretary of State while remaining National Security Adviser. Nixon and Kissinger shared the same geopolitical vision. Both were strongly anti-Communist but focused less on the ideological battle and more on responding to Soviet power. Their first priority was to extricate the country from Vietnam. They wanted to stem the growing tide of opposition to American involvement in Vietnam by reducing US troop levels, and they felt they could achieve this by ending Chinese and Soviet support for North Vietnam. They calculated that both Moscow and Beijing might be willing to disengage in return for better relations with Washington. This 'triangular diplomacy' lay at the heart of the Nixon-Kissinger strategy.

West Germany also wished to put its relations with the Eastern bloc on a new basis. In October 1969 Willy Brandt became chancellor and pursued an *Ostpolitik* (Eastern policy) of economic and cultural interchanges between East and West and the formalization of borders. He concluded the West Germany-USSR Non-Aggression

President Richard Nixon and advisers in the Oval Office. Henry Kissinger stands at the left.

West German Chancellor Willy Brandt kneeling before the Jewish Heroes Monument in Warsaw, 7 December 1970, paying tribute to Jews killed by Nazis in the 1943 Warsaw Ghetto uprising.

Pact in August 1970. The December 1970 treaty with Poland recognized the Oder-Neisse frontier between the two countries and renounced any future German territorial claims. In a memorable gesture, Brandt knelt in penitence at the memorial to the Warsaw Ghetto. Finally, Brandt proposed a non-aggression pact between the two German states, but the offer did not involve full diplomatic recognition and so was rejected by East Germany.

These talks ran in parallel with discussions on Berlin, begun in March 1970, between the four occupying powers (Britain, France, the Soviet Union and the United States). But Brandt would not ratify the Moscow and Warsaw treaties until there was agreement on Berlin.

The Berlin Agreement of 3 September 1971 guaranteed Western access to the city. The Soviets accepted the legality of political ties between Berlin and Bonn, and so Brandt agreed to lessen West Germany's political role in Berlin. The West recognized East Germany (GDR) and the Soviets accepted the continuation of the four powers' responsibilities for Berlin. GDR-West German transit agreements were reached and, in December 1972, a 'Treaty on the Bases of Relations' was concluded. The two German states recognized one another, renounced the use of force and committed themselves to increased trade and travel between the two countries.

Nixon and Kissinger feared that Brandt's Ostpolitik might drive a wedge between West Germany and the United States. In the event, they were pleased with the results of Brandt's diplomacy, especially on Berlin, and they decided to develop their own policy of détente. Their priority, however, remained to end US involvement in Vietnam, but to do so in a way that did not look like a defeat. Nixon accepted that this meant a reduced world role for America. In July 1969 he announced what became known as the Nixon Doctrine: American air and naval forces would uphold treaty obligations in the western Pacific, but Asian troops would assume the principal responsibility on the ground as American troops withdrew. Nixon and Kissinger reduced US troop numbers in Vietnam from approximately 540,000 in 1969 to roughly 160,000 in December 1971. They shifted the military burden to the South Vietnamese government, supporting this 'Vietnamization' policy with $1 billion of weapons and matériel for the South in 1969.

Formal peace talks between the US, North Vietnam and South Vietnam began in Paris in January 1969, although serious discussion only started in August with secret meetings between Kissinger and the senior North Vietnamese negotiator, Xuan Thuy, later succeeded by Le Duc Tho. Nixon and Kissinger hoped for a face-saving withdrawal, but there was little progress until Kissinger abandoned his stipulation that both US and North Vietnamese forces should withdraw from the South; he then proposed a ceasefire leaving South and North Vietnamese forces in their existing positions. North Vietnam, however, still hoped to win on the battlefield and launched a major offensive in May 1972. Despite initial success, this was comprehensively defeated, after which the North returned to negotiations.

OPPOSITE Henry Kissinger and Le Duc Tho sign the Vietnam ceasefire agreement, Paris, 23 January 1973.

A draft agreement in October 1972 between Kissinger and Le Duc Tho involved a total withdrawal of American air, land and naval forces from Vietnam, a ceasefire in the South that would leave North and South Vietnamese forces in their existing positions, and a commitment to future democratic elections on whether South Vietnam remained independent or would reunite with the North. The South Vietnamese leader Nguyen Van Thieu rejected the draft treaty. Deeply frustrated, Nixon resumed the bombing of North Vietnam to demonstrate both to Thieu and to the North Vietnamese what the United States could do if the peace treaty were to be broken by the North. This persuaded Thieu, who agreed to sign the final peace treaty – unchanged from the October draft agreement – in Paris on 23 January 1973. The war was finally over, but it had cost 58,000 American lives and perhaps two million Vietnamese deaths.

The treaty was not in fact a direct result of 'triangular diplomacy', as Nixon and Kissinger liked to believe. China and the Soviet

Union wanted an end to the war but did not press their fellow Communists to accept any settlement. Success was due partly to the substantial US concessions, but also to the North's concern about its own weakened military position after the failure of its May 1972 assault, in the face of the expected revival (as the American threat dissipated) of its regional rivalries with China over Laos and Cambodia.

The Nixon-Kissinger strategy had a more direct impact on improving relations with China and the Soviet Union, aiming to exploit the deepening Sino-Soviet split – there was serious fighting on the Ussuri River between March and September 1969. Nixon calculated that the Chinese, anxious about Soviet intentions, would welcome better relations with Washington as a counterbalance, so he made gestures designed to encourage an easing of contacts. After July 1969 American students and scholars no longer required special permission for visits to China. In October the US ambassador to Poland proposed talks between Chinese and American diplomats in Warsaw. China then invited an American journalist, Edgar Snow (author of the 1937 book *Red Star Over China*), to its National Day celebrations in October 1970. Mao told Snow of his concerns about the Sino-Soviet conflict and spoke more favourably of the United States. In April 1971 the Chinese sent a very public signal by inviting the American table tennis team to China. Meanwhile, secret exchanges through Pakistan led to a Chinese invitation for the United States to send an envoy to Beijing. Kissinger visited Pakistan in July 1971 and, feigning illness, spent two days in Beijing during which the Chinese invited Nixon to visit China. The American public then heard the astonishing news that Nixon would go to China. In October 1971 Communist China replaced Nationalist China (Taiwan) at the UN, which removed a major barrier to better US-Chinese relations.

Although it was largely symbolic, Nixon's February 1972 visit to China was a huge success. It removed much of the bitterness that had existed in Sino-American relations since Mao's victory in 1949. The Americans continued to guarantee Taiwan's security, but diplomats devised a compromise formula: the Chinese claim to Taiwan was conceded, and a settlement would be pursued by peaceful means. In a further trip to Beijing in 1973 Kissinger established an American liaison office, an embassy in all but name. On this foundation US-Chinese relations continued to improve for nearly two decades.

Ping-pong diplomacy: American and Chinese table tennis players in Beijing, April 1971.

President Nixon in China, February 1972, enjoying the view from the Great Wall.

Nixon deserves the major credit for this achievement: he conceived the idea and played an important part in its implementation. But he had an advantage in pursuing this policy. His fierce anti-Communism undercut accusations by the political right in America that he was being soft on Communism, a charge that would almost certainly have defeated such a policy if proposed by a liberal Democratic president. Yet, for all its benefits for Sino-American relations, Nixon's main objective was not to support China against the Soviet Union but to encourage a more accommodating attitude by the Soviet Union towards the United States.

In June 1969 Nixon decided to revive the SALT conversations begun by Johnson. The Soviets were initially hesitant but agreed to a preliminary meeting in Helsinki in November–December 1969. However, it was only after the opening of diplomatic relations between the United States and China that serious negotiations started. Nixon and Brezhnev held three summit meetings: Moscow in May 1972, Washington in June 1973, and Moscow in June–July 1974. They discussed issues ranging from arms control to trade, from cultural, scientific and educational ties to ways of dealing with potential tensions.

The SALT I agreement on strategic nuclear weapons of May 1972 imposed a five-year freeze on US and Soviet missile launchers: 1,054 American to 1,618 Soviet ICBMs; 656 American submarine-launched ballistic missiles (SLBMs) to 740 Soviet ones; and 455 American to 140 Soviet long-range bombers. This gave the Soviets an advantage in launcher numbers, but the Americans had developed Multiple Independently Targetable Re-entry Vehicles (MIRVs) and thus enjoyed an estimated three to one superiority in warheads. So the Soviets began developing their own MIRVs, leading to another arms race. SALT I, therefore, did not significantly reduce armaments, but it marked the beginning of a readiness to try to apply common controls. In addition, the two powers concluded an anti-ABM Treaty,

Richard Nixon and Leonid
Brezhnev exchanging
copies of the SALT I
agreement in Moscow,
26 May 1972.

which allowed two ABM systems (of 100 missiles) for each country – to be positioned around Moscow and Washington and at a selected missile site. Nixon and Brezhnev also signed a Joint Declaration on Basic Principles, which committed them to consult one another in order to avoid an escalation of tensions, and the spirit of cooperation was reinforced by a number of economic agreements. SALT I was to run for five years: the aim was to seek an improved agreement in SALT II talks.

W87
MX MISSILE

The ending of the US involvement in Vietnam, the Sino-American rapprochement and the US-Soviet SALT I agreements all contributed to an easing of Cold War tensions. But there was a fragile quality to each of these achievements; America seemed less assured after the experience of Vietnam. In addition, the period of economic growth in the West since 1945 was coming to an end. The prospects for the future appeared unclear.

Chapter 5

Bleak Midwinter: 1972–1983

It proved difficult after 1972 to build on the achievements of détente. The opening to China did not remove sharp ideological differences or the disagreement over Taiwan, whose US supporters criticized Nixon's policy and argued against further accommodation with Beijing. There was growing criticism of SALT for conceding too much to the Soviets. The situation was not helped by Brezhnev's deteriorating health. The Vietnam peace settlement also began to unravel. Above all, the United States in the early 1970s saw the enthusiasm and, at times, near euphoria of the 1960s give way to gloomy assessments of the nation's place in the world. Overshadowing everything was defeat in the Vietnam War, and rising rates of divorce, illegitimacy and violent crime added to the national despondency. Furthermore, US economic predominance also seemed under threat. Unemployment rose from 3.6 per cent in 1968 to 5.6 per cent in 1972, while consumer prices increased by about 20 per cent in the same period. The early 1970s saw this combination of rising prices and higher unemployment across the Western world – analysts talked of 'stagflation'. In 1971 the United States registered its first negative balance of international trade since 1893, as the country faced increasing competition from West Germany and, above all, Japan. Books such as Ezra F. Vogel's *Japan as Number One: Lessons for America* (1979) predicted Japan's imminent replacement of the US as the world's strongest economy. There was also a mushrooming federal budget deficit as a result of increased social spending and the vast costs of the Vietnam War. So large was the outflow of dollars for

OPPOSITE US gasoline shortage, 1973.

imports and Vietnam that Nixon decided on 15 August 1971 to end the policy under which the dollar was convertible into gold.

In these circumstances the Americans and Soviets struggled to make progress on SALT II, and then an international crisis arose in the Middle East. On 6 October 1973 (Yom Kippur, the Jewish Day of Atonement) the Egyptians and Syrians launched an attack on Israel. Ever since Kennedy began supplying arms to Israel and promised aid if it was a victim of aggression, the US-Israel alliance had been growing. Anxious about the initial Israeli losses, Washington mounted a major resupply programme that turned the tide for Israel. Facing the prospect of defeat, Egypt and Syria appealed to the Soviets for help, which led to Brezhnev and Kissinger arranging a ceasefire agreement.

Bretton Woods

Convinced that the worldwide economic depression had contributed to the outbreak of the Second World War, forty-five nations (including the USSR, which later opted out) met at Bretton Woods, New Hampshire in July 1944 to create a more stable global economic framework. They aimed to establish stable currencies, which would avoid competitive devaluations, and a reliable regime of international payments.

They set up the International Monetary Fund (IMF) to provide short-term finance to overcome payment difficulties and the World Bank to offer loans for longer-term projects such as transport systems.

Since the Americans provided the bulk of the funding for these institutions, they dominated them. The conference participants also adopted fixed exchange rates, pegged against the dollar, redeemable in gold at $35 an ounce. It was only after 1958 that the countries of the Western world progressively made their currencies freely convertible.

The system worked well until the 1960s, when US debts mounted as a result of vast Vietnam War expenditure and the rise of imports from West Germany and Japan. When Japan refused to revalue its currency to ease the outflow of dollars, America abandoned the policy of convertibility into gold and devalued the dollar. After 1973 most countries adopted floating currencies.

Delegates from forty-four nations at the Bretton Woods conference, 2 July 1944.

ABOVE Israeli Defence Minister Moshe Dayan overseeing the advance against Syria, 18 October 1973.

LEFT Egyptian troops holding up a picture of President Anwar Sadat during the Yom Kippur War with Israel, October 1973.

Kissinger, however, secretly approved Israel's delayed implementation of the ceasefire. This infuriated the Egyptian leader, Anwar Sadat, who called for troops from the major powers to enforce the armistice. Brezhnev endorsed his idea, saying that if the Americans did not contribute to a joint force, then the Soviet Union would consider acting alone. Washington regarded this as an ultimatum, though Brezhnev probably meant only to put pressure on the Americans to act. On

Oil storage in Yemen, 1970.

24 October United States forces around the world were placed on Defense Condition III, the highest state of preparedness short of war. This did not develop into a more serious crisis partly because the fighting ended and partly due to Brezhnev's restraint. Yet for a while it was the most serious episode of US-Soviet tension since the Cuban missile crisis.

The Middle East had become a vital region for the United States because of its alliance with Israel and even more because of its growing need of oil from the area. The Organization of Petroleum Exporting Countries (OPEC) exploited this as a means of backing the Egyptians and Syrians, increasing the price of oil by 70 per cent and imposing a boycott on the United States. OPEC only removed its oil embargo after Kissinger had negotiated disengagement agreements between Israel and both Egypt and Syria. But the price of oil remained high: Saudi light crude had risen from $2.18 a barrel in January 1971 to $11.65 a barrel in December 1973. The era of cheap oil, which had helped to fuel American economic growth since the 1940s, was over. The sudden steep price rises produced inflation, which was already being stoked by the huge increases in defence spending required to fight the Vietnam War.

The United States and Israel

The United States has been closely associated with Israel since the Jewish state was created in 1948. Truman immediately recognized the new nation despite the opposition of his Secretary of State, George Marshall. Washington may have allowed American sympathizers to help the Israelis, but it was determined not to provide official military assistance to Israel. Policymakers understood how this would antagonize the Arabs who controlled large reserves of oil, which was becoming increasingly important to the US. This policy was maintained until arms were sent from the Soviet bloc to Egypt in 1955, resulting in Eisenhower's decision to send US weapons to Israel: Cold War rivalry had reached the Middle East. Nevertheless, Eisenhower restricted American military aid.

By the early 1960s, however, the Soviets were supplying tanks and bombers and the West Germans were sending missiles to Egypt. So Kennedy approved the despatch of surface-to-air (SAM) missiles to Israel – the first

time the Americans had provided a major weapons system. Johnson extended the flow of weapons with tanks and planes, and Nixon insisted on resupplying the Israelis during the 1973 Yom Kippur War. The Americans were unwilling to see the defeat of Israel, which they felt would be deemed a victory for the Soviets.

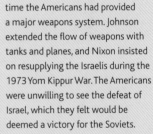

ABOVE *Israeli F-15 fighter during combat training with the US Air Force at the Nevada Test and Training Ranges.*

LEFT *Arrow anti-ballistic missile launch (part of the US/Israel Arrow System Improvement Program), 29 July 2004.*

Nixon's handling of the October (Yom Kippur) War was undoubtedly hindered by a major political crisis confronting his administration at home. In June 1972 burglars broke into and placed electronic bugs in the Democratic Party's National Committee headquarters in the Watergate building in Washington, DC. Nixon almost certainly did not order or even know about the burglary personally, but the break-in was a symptom of his administration's paranoia. The scandal only broke after Nixon's re-election in November 1972. In 1973 the burglars spoke to prosecutors, investigative journalists Bob Woodward and Carl Bernstein of *The Washington Post* pursued the story, and an independent special prosecutor was appointed. A Senate Committee chaired by Sam Ervin (Democrat from North Carolina) was established and its hearings were broadcast live on television. In July a White House aide revealed that Nixon taped his conversations. For the next year Congress sought these recordings until, in July 1974, the Supreme Court ordered Nixon to release them. One transcript contained Nixon's order to his chief of staff, H. R. Haldeman, to arrange for the FBI to halt its inquiry into the Watergate burglary. Facing the prospect of impeachment by Congress, Nixon decided to resign on 9 August, addressing his brief letter to Henry Kissinger as Secretary of State.

Richard Nixon leaving the White House on 9 August 1974; the new President, Gerald Ford, is on the left.

Vice-President Gerald Ford succeeded Richard Nixon as president. He allowed Kissinger to take the lead in foreign policy, and his full pardon to Nixon damaged his reputation – many assumed it was part of a prior deal. He also inherited a host of difficulties. First came the collapse of the Vietnam peace settlement, as both sides violated the agreement by continuing military operations. Following Watergate, Congress blocked US military action in the region, cut aid to South Vietnam from $2.3 billion in 1973 to $700 million by November 1974, and, in November 1973, passed the War Powers Act, which placed a sixty-day limit on troop deployments overseas without Congressional approval. The North Vietnamese went on to invade and defeat the South. By 30 April 1975 they occupied Saigon and quickly established a single Communist government. Communists had taken control of Cambodia in January 1975 and Laos followed in August, leaving all of Indochina in Communist hands.

Ford then faced the assertion of Soviet power in Africa. Moscow believed that détente only applied to Europe, for the Americans were

The fall of Saigon: South Vietnamese evacuees board an Air America helicopter, 29 April 1975.

continuing to pursue their interests in other regions. In April 1974 a military coup brought a new government in Portugal, which granted independence to its African colonies. In the civil war that followed in Angola, Cuban troops and Soviet military aid helped put the Popular Movement for the Liberation of Angola (MPLA) in power in March 1976. Angola then started supporting the South West Africa People's Organization (SWAPO) guerrillas in their fight to take control of Namibia from South Africa. Ford and Kissinger were worried about what they saw as the use of 'proxies' to extend Soviet influence on the continent. But Congress would not support another Third World intervention.

Despite these setbacks, there was at least one success in East-West détente. The Conference on Security and Co-operation in Europe (CSCE) talks in 1972–75 produced the Helsinki Final Act of August 1975, which contained three broad agreements known as

Our position is we want a political solution which does not guarantee a Communist victory, but also, we emphasize, we don't exclude it.

Kissinger to Gromyko about doing a deal on Vietnam, May 1972[1]

baskets. In basket I the signatories recognized the postwar European frontiers and committed themselves to greater exchanges of military information. In basket II they agreed to greater economic, scientific and technological cooperation. In basket III they pledged themselves to allow closer contacts between peoples and greater respect for human rights. The Helsinki Accords gave the Soviets the recognition of 1945 borders that they wanted. But they also had to accept clauses on human rights that were to prove a very effective mechanism for criticism of Soviet rule by Warsaw Pact citizens.

Because the Soviets were initially successful in repressing dissident groups, criticism of the Helsinki Accords and détente in general continued to grow. Senator Henry 'Scoop' Jackson (Democrat from Washington) maintained that US-Soviet economic agreements should be tied to the Soviet performance on human rights. Kissinger became the focus of criticism, leading Ford to remove him from the post of National Security Adviser in December 1975. During the 1976 presidential election détente was attacked from the Republican right by Ronald Reagan, who claimed that Ford had negotiated away US nuclear superiority and legitimized Soviet dominance of Eastern Europe. Jimmy Carter, the Democratic candidate, charged the Ford and Nixon administrations with lacking a moral dimension to their policies.

Further advance on SALT also stalled. In November 1974 Ford and Brezhnev held a summit in Vladivostock on a framework for SALT II: an equal limit of 2,400 missiles or bombers on each side,

Gerald Ford and Leonid Brezhnev sign a joint statement on SALT II in Vladivostock, 24 November 1974.

Anwar Sadat, Jimmy Carter and Menachem Begin at Camp David, 1978.

with no more than 1,320 of them to have MIRV capability. But the combination of technical disagreements on weapons and American domestic criticism prevented progress.

Ford lost the 1976 presidential election to Jimmy Carter, who had campaigned as an outsider untouched by Watergate or the claims of CIA involvement in the coup against Salvador Allende in Chile in September 1973. Carter entered office determined to eschew the power politics of Nixon, Ford and Kissinger, but this proved much more difficult than he had expected. Nevertheless, he did enjoy two successes. The first came when he concluded an agreement on the Panama Canal in 1977, in which legal control of the Canal Zone would return to Panama after 31 December 1999; until then, the United States would operate and defend the canal. The Canal Zone would be neutralized, but the United States retained the right to protect the 'neutrality of the waterway'.

The Carter administration also brokered a peace treaty between Israel and Egypt. The breakthrough came when the Egyptian leader Anwar Sadat visited Jerusalem and told the Israeli Parliament in November 1977 that he was ready 'to live with you in permanent peace based on justice'.[2] Carter hosted a two-week summit at Camp David in September 1978 between Sadat and the Israeli leader Menachem Begin. Sadat agreed to a separate peace treaty with Israel, but Begin refused to include the issue of Palestine in the treaty, agreeing only to further conversations on the future of the West Bank.

STOP RUSSIAN AND CUBAN AGGRESSION IN THE HORN OF AFRI

A further six months of pressure, cajolery and promises of aid from the Americans were required before Sadat, Begin and Carter signed the peace treaty on the White House lawn on 26 March 1979.

Such achievements did little to ease the problems in US-Soviet relations, however, which surfaced again in Africa. In July 1977 Somalia invaded the disputed Ogaden region of Ethiopia, forcing the Soviets to choose between their two allies. They decided to back Ethiopia, which led Somalia to obtain US military aid. Moscow sent armaments, 15,000 Cuban troops and 1,000 Soviet advisers to Ethiopia, and as a result the Somalis were defeated and withdrew.

Although there was no escalation, the Soviet intervention worried the Americans. They were also concerned over intermediate-range nuclear missiles in Europe. Brezhnev had agreed at Vladivostock to exclude the British and French nuclear weapons from the SALT II talks. But his military persuaded him to develop SS-20s to replace SS-4s and SS-5s, which might then be used in bargaining if the Americans developed Cruise missiles (low-level radar-evading nuclear weapons). In 1977 the Soviets began deploying SS-20s in Eastern Europe, and the Americans considered deploying their own intermediate-range missiles in Western Europe.

Carter's National Security Adviser Zbigniew Brzezinski convinced the president that they could strengthen their position with the Soviet Union if they pursued better relations with Beijing. China sought American technology and expertise to aid its modernization and was worried about the Soviet alliance with Vietnam. In March 1979 they each established an embassy in the other's capital. The Americans agreed to end their defence treaty and 'official' relations with Taiwan, while the Chinese undertook not to invade the island. January 1979 witnessed the first visit to the United States of a senior Chinese Communist, Vice-Premier Deng Xiaoping. The new friendship was undisturbed by Chinese military action against Vietnam in February, which was undertaken both to demonstrate their backing for Kampuchea (formerly Cambodia) and to assert their role in the region.

Progress in US-Soviet relations was less smooth. The Carter administration appeared, at first, to accept the SALT II terms agreed by Ford at Vladivostock. Carter then told Brezhnev of his wish for lower ceilings, but Soviet anger forced him to return to the Vladivostock terms. Negotiations produced a Final Treaty, signed by Carter and Brezhnev in June 1979. There would be equal ceilings of 2,400 strategic nuclear weapon launchers or heavy bombers, which would fall to 2,250 by 1985. No more than 1,320 of these could be either MIRVs or air-launched Cruise missiles. As many as 1,200 launchers could be MIRVs, while up to 820 of these MIRVs could be on ICBMs. The Soviets ratified the treaty soon after the summit. The terms of SALT II were a significant improvement on those of its predecessor: they established numerical equality, restricted MIRVs and committed (but did not compel) the two powers to cut their missile numbers.

Soviet SS-20 intermediate-range ballistic missile.

Although SALT II was a real achievement, it suffered from continued criticism within the United States. Many in the Senate complained that it did not halt the growth of Soviet military power. The Committee on the Present Danger, a political lobbying group, was revived in 1976 (it was originally formed in 1950 to press for increased military expenditure). Its members included the Republican right as well as neo-conservatives – ex-liberals who felt the Democratic Party underestimated the threat of Communism. Some critics felt SALT II did not reduce nuclear weapons sufficiently, while others wanted to tie the treaty to the Soviet record on human rights. Although Congress never ratified SALT II, the two signatories nevertheless agreed, in 1980, to abide by the terms of the treaty, which was to last until 1985.

Ratification was hindered by crises in Iran and Afghanistan. On 11 February 1979 revolutionaries overthrew the Iranian monarchy and established an Islamic republic. The revolution resulted in another oil crisis for the West, as Iranian production fell by 90 per cent and the price of oil rose from $18 to $36 a barrel. Long queues for gasoline at American filling stations generated growing criticism of Carter. The Islamic revolutionaries were deeply anti-American –

American motorists
queuing for gasoline,
1979.

50,000 Americans worked in the Shah's Iran, which was known to have received strong support from Washington dating as far back as the coup against Mossadeq in 1953. When Carter allowed the Shah to come to the United States for medical treatment, the new Iranian leader, Ayatollah Khomeini, encouraged his followers on to the streets. On 4 November 1979 they attacked the US embassy in Tehran and seized fifty-six Americans (fifty-two of these hostages were not released until January 1981, after a long series of negotiations and an abortive rescue attempt in April 1980). All this hurt American pride and led to calls for more aggressive policies.

US anxieties deepened when the Soviets invaded Afghanistan on 25 December 1979, seeing it as another threat to a strategically important region. Soviet intervention was probably motivated by fear that the ruling Communist People's Democratic Party of Afghanistan would be succeeded by another fundamentalist Islamic state on its borders. The Americans, however, detected offensive intent: Carter described the invasion as a 'quantum leap in the nature of Soviet behavior'. He withdrew the SALT II treaty from the Senate, halted the sale of American grain and high-technology equipment to the Soviet Union and declared a boycott of the 1980 Moscow Olympics. In his

Afghan Mujahedeen fighters in Asmar, Afghanistan, January 1980.

State of the Union speech in January 1980 he enunciated what became known as the Carter Doctrine: the United States would repel 'by any means, including military force' any external power seeking to secure control of the Persian Gulf.[3] He also promised to increase defence spending by 5 per cent in real terms each year for the next five years. Thus the Carter presidency, despite its aspirations to the contrary, ended with an intensified Cold War between the United States and the Soviet Union.

These new strains in US-Soviet relations appeared likely to increase when the right-wing Republican Ronald Reagan defeated Carter in the 1980 presidential election. Reagan favoured reducing the scope of government and cutting taxes. Above all, he wanted to resist what he saw as the evil of Communism. He would avoid deals that consolidated Soviet power, build up US military strength and offer assistance to anti-Communist movements around the world.

Reagan had to frame his policies in difficult economic circumstances. There were the inflationary effects of the steep rises in oil prices, which also caused large external deficits. In 1980–81 there was a sharp global recession. Reagan cut taxes but also adopted a programme of increased defence expenditure, convinced that American power had declined relative to that of the Soviet Union. In fact, SALT

B-2 Stealth bomber on its first public flight, September 2007.

Sandinista guerrillas arrive in the Nicaraguan capital, Managua, after the resignation of dictator Anastasio Somoza, 19 July 1979.

II gave the United States a 50 per cent advantage in strategic nuclear warheads, but in 1974 the Americans had possessed a three-to-one advantage. Reagan set a five-year defence budget of $1.6 trillion ($400 million greater than Carter's increases) – the largest peacetime military build-up in US history. The Soviet leadership became alarmed at what they took to be an American attempt to develop a first-strike capability.

Reagan also increased funds to the CIA, especially for its support of anti-Communist guerrillas in Afghanistan, Angola and Cambodia. In addition, Central America was a particular focus for assistance. American military advisers helped the government of El Salvador resist a Communist threat. However, US aid failed to bring the Contras victory over the Sandinista government in Nicaragua. Even worse, a scandal was to break over clandestine support for the

Contras. In October 1986 it was revealed that Robert McFarlane, the National Security Adviser, had reached a deal to sell military parts to Iran (which it was banned from receiving) in return for help in releasing Americans abducted in Lebanon and for passing the money to the Contras. An investigation censured the administration and the National Security Council (NSC) in particular, but it did not find the president personally culpable.

Reagan's approach to the Soviets was to await the restoration of American military power before beginning talks: he favoured negotiation from a position of strength. He did not meet Ambassador Dobrynin until February 1983, while the first discussions with the Soviet foreign minister, Andrei Gromyko, took place in September 1984. He renamed the SALT negotiations as the Strategic Arms Reductions Talks (START) to convey his commitment to reductions rather than just limitations, but there were no formal US-Soviet discussions until June 1982. The focus, instead, was on Intermediate Nuclear Forces (INF). The Soviets had been deploying SS-20s since 1977, and in December 1979 NATO decided to deploy American Cruise and Pershing II missiles in Europe in response. Many in Western Europe were concerned about the arrival of new nuclear missiles, especially when the US administration was employing fiercely anti-Communist rhetoric. Widespread protest in Western Europe was

Women, including many supporters of CND (Campaign for Nuclear Disarmament), join hands outside the RAF base at Greenham Common in Berkshire, protesting against the presence of US Cruise missiles in Britain.

Lech Walesa is carried on the shoulders of a crowd of supporters after the Polish Supreme Court allowed registration of Peasant Solidarity, 1980.

expressed in mass demonstrations numbering tens of thousands. In October 1981 marches in London, Rome and Bonn each brought out over 250,000 people. The Soviets hoped to exploit this opposition to prevent the deployment.

Formal INF talks began in Geneva in November 1981 but were soon overwhelmed by events in Poland. In 1978 John Paul II had become the first Polish pope. He visited Poland in 1979 and encouraged opposition groups, which led to the creation in 1980 of Solidarity, an independent, non-Communist trade union. Under the

The fact that we represent hundreds of thousands of people makes us feel that the cause we are fighting for is just. Coming here may make you understand what a shipyard is like when the workers are governing themselves. You can see for yourself how orderly it all is.

Lech Walesa in talks with Polish Communist Party officials about the Solidarity movement in the Gdansk shipyards,

23 August 1980[4]

leadership of Lech Walesa it became a significant political movement in Poland. Moscow feared the collapse of the Communist regime and pressed General Wojciech Jaruzelski to introduce martial law in December 1981. Despite this backdrop and being far apart in their original positions, the INF negotiators reached a provisional agreement in July 1982: the Soviets could deploy 75 SS-20s and the Americans could deploy 75 Cruise missiles but no Pershing missiles. However, neither Moscow nor Washington wanted to convert this into a binding arrangement, leaving deadlock in both the INF and START talks.

Pope John Paul II enters the gates of Auschwitz concentration camp in Poland, 7 June 1979.

In 1983 US-Soviet relations deteriorated still further. On 23 March Reagan announced the Strategic Defense Initiative (SDI) programme, soon known as 'Star Wars': a proposal for a protective screen of lasers or particle beam weapons in space to shoot down incoming nuclear missiles. Although most scientists regarded it as an expensive fantasy, it disturbed the Soviets. After all, if it worked, it would undermine their nuclear deterrent. Reagan's rhetoric exacerbated the situation – in a speech in Florida he referred to the Soviet Union as an 'evil empire'.[5] Mutual recriminations deepened when, in September, a Soviet fighter plane shot down a Korean Airlines flight (KAL 007) en route from Alaska to Seoul, South Korea, killing all 269 people on board. As a result of faulty navigation it entered Soviet air space, and the Soviets probably assumed it was an American spy plane. The Reagan administration condemned the action in strong terms, calling it an 'act of barbarism',[6] but Moscow was unapologetic.

Moscow now harboured growing suspicions of American intentions. Yuri Andropov, who had become Communist Party leader after Brezhnev's death in November 1982, spoke of the 'militarist course' of the United States. Oleg Gordievsky, working as a British double agent in the KGB, reported that Andropov had believed since 1981 that the Americans were preparing for a nuclear war. He seems to have regarded the American invasion of the Caribbean island of Grenada in October 1983 as a worrying portent. Reagan wanted to remove the Marxist government that had seized power in a bloody coup, lest the almost 1,000 Americans on the island were caught up in another

Ronald Reagan introduces the Strategic Defense Initiative in a speech from the Oval Office, March 1983.

hostage crisis like the one in Iran. The Soviets detected further aggressiveness in the NATO exercise 'Able Archer' in November, which led Moscow on 8–9 November to warn its missions abroad that American bases had been placed on alert. In the same month the deployment of Cruise and Pershing II missiles began in Europe.

Artist's impression of SDI weapons system, 1984.

East-West relations had reached new depths in mutual suspicion and no mechanisms seemed in place to ameliorate the situation. In November 1983 the Soviets quit the INF talks and left the START discussions the following month. For the first time in fifteen years, the Americans and Soviets were not even talking to one another.

Chapter 6

Endings: 1983–1991

US-Soviet relations seemed at a dangerous point of confrontation in late 1983. The Reagan administration denounced the evils of Communism and pursued massive increases in defence expenditure. The elderly and ailing Soviet leadership appeared ill-prepared to respond, harbouring deep suspicions of American intentions. The Soviet Union also faced growing economic problems: the steep rises in oil and gas prices since 1973 had boosted Soviet overseas earnings from exports of these commodities, but prices began to fall back in the early 1980s. Popular culture reflected the anxieties. In Britain Raymond Briggs's graphic novel (1982) and animated film (1986), *When the Wind Blows*, recounted an elderly couple's attempts to apply the British government's patently inadequate advice to citizens as the country experiences a nuclear attack. The American movie *Red Dawn* (1984) told the story of a group of Midwestern resisters to a Soviet invasion of the United States.

Yet late 1983 and early 1984 also saw more encouraging signs. Reagan had shown a greater readiness to avoid confrontation than his public rhetoric might have suggested. In April 1981 he had written to Brezhnev seeking 'meaningful and constructive dialogue'. These inclinations were reinforced in late 1983 by Oleg Gordievsky, who had spied for Britain's MI6 and had since defected, and who told

OPPOSITE A demonstrator takes a hammer to the Berlin Wall as East German border guards look on, 11 November 1989.

I urge you to speak out against those who would place the United States in a position of military and moral inferiority [and not] ignore the facts of history and the aggressive impulses of an evil empire.

Ronald Reagan, speech to National Association of Evangelicals, Orlando, Florida, 8 March 1983[1]

the Americans about the Soviet fears of a US attack. As Reagan recorded in his memoirs, 'Many people at the top of the Soviet hierarchy were genuinely afraid of America and the Americans. Perhaps this shouldn't have surprised me but it did.… Soviet officials feared us not only as adversaries but as potential aggressors who might hurl nuclear weapons at them in a first strike.'[2] Some historians think Reagan was also influenced by the large-scale peace protests.

Hardline anti-Communists within the administration, especially Secretary of Defense Caspar Weinberger, resisted the reopening of talks. Reagan, however, wanted to meet a senior Soviet leader 'in a room alone and try and convince him that we had no designs on the Soviet Union'.[3] In pursuing this goal he was greatly aided by Secretary of State George Shultz. Reagan ordered Shultz to form a small group that would seek new channels of communication with the Kremlin. Shultz felt the time was opportune, because the deployment of Cruise and Pershing II missiles in Europe in November 1983 gave the Americans bargaining strength from which to begin negotiations.

During 1984 Reagan publicly declared his more open approach. In January he spoke of Jim and Sally and Ivan and Anya, two couples who both yearned for peace. On 24 September he brought to the UN General Assembly new proposals for US-Soviet talks on START, INF and, a new area, anti-satellite weapons (ASAT). Four days later he met Gromyko, who was, in Reagan's words, as 'hard as granite' but gave the impression that the Soviets might return to talks following the November US presidential election.[4] After Reagan won in November, the Soviets agreed to talks under that framework. Shultz and Gromyko met in January 1985 and agreed to begin discussions in March. But that month saw the death of Konstantin Chernenko, who had succeeded Andropov as Communist Party General Secretary in February 1984.

The death of another Soviet leader did not prove a setback. Indeed it proved to be fortuitous, for Chernenko's successor was the talented and dynamic fifty-four-year-old Mikhail Gorbachev. He appointed Eduard Shevardnadze, First Secretary of the Communist Party in Georgia, to replace Gromyko as foreign minister. Shultz was impressed with Shevardnadze: 'He could smile, engage, converse. He had an ability to persuade and to be persuaded. We were in a real diplomatic competition now.'[5]

US Secretary of State George P. Shultz.

The Soviet Economy

The precipitous collapse of the Soviet economy in the late 1980s greatly surprised many observers in the West. Here was a country with vast tracts of fertile land, huge reserves of oil and gas and other raw materials, industries capable of producing sophisticated weapons, and large numbers of gifted scientists and mathematicians.

Most economic activity, however, served military needs (between a sixth and a quarter of the national budget) at the expense of other parts of the economy, especially agriculture. Khrushchev tried to direct more resources to consumer goods and housing but faced resistance from the military and heads of heavy industry.

There were deepening structural problems: an inflexible command economy was run by an inefficient and frequently corrupt bureaucracy; a country with extensive agricultural land needed to import grain; exports were over-dependent on oil and gas; and population growth was declining (1 per cent in the early 1980s). Above all, the country was slipping behind technologically. By the 1980s there was zero economic growth.

Observers were distracted by the military power on display and the lack of accurate statistics. Intelligence agencies were hindered by the consequences of getting their evaluations wrong – it was generally considered safer to assume their adversary was strong.

Queuing for shoes in Moscow, 1987.

Gorbachev inherited considerable difficulties. The war in Afghanistan was proving a costly failure. The steadily improving US-Chinese relationship made the Soviets feel more isolated internationally. Above all, he was faced with an inefficient and corrupt command economy registering zero economic growth while defence spending had reached a sixth, perhaps even a quarter, of GDP. The more urbanized (65 per cent in 1985, compared to 49 per cent in 1960) and educated populace were less willing to accept shortages, especially since they coincided with a surge in economic growth in the United States and Western Europe and the rise of the Asian 'tiger' economies. Technological advances, in particular the revolution in computers and communications, left the Soviet bloc still further behind economically, and Moscow also confronted growing dissident movements.

Gorbachev was confident he could revitalize the Communist system. He began a programme of public debates to identify problems. The Government would pursue *perestroika* (restructuring) and do this through *glasnost* (greater openness). Together with Shevardnadze, Gorbachev adopted a similarly optimistic approach to international relations. He impressed the British prime minister, Margaret Thatcher, who declared after meeting him in December 1984, before he became the Soviet leader: 'I like Mr Gorbachev. We can do business together.' He also made a favourable impression on

The Cold War and Latin America

The United States has traditionally opposed the intrusion of other powers into the Americas, and during the Cold War this meant resisting the spread of Communism. Many postcolonial dictatorships throughout Central and South America were heavily dependent on US private investment as well as military aid, and the divide between the very rich and very poor was great. Left-wing opposition to American-backed governments often advocated redistribution of land and nationalization of major industries, and US fears became sharper after Khrushchev announced Soviet support for 'national liberation' movements across the globe; the US-built Panama Canal made Central America a particular concern.

Washington used a combination of diplomatic pressure, economic aid, and both overt and covert military assistance. In 1954 Eisenhower approved a CIA-led military coup in Guatemala, and in 1973 Nixon condoned the military overthrow of the elected Allende Socialist government in Chile.

Cuba assumed a central importance in American policy after the defeat of the Batista regime by Fidel Castro in 1959. Castro received Soviet aid and, fearing that the Cubans would seek to export Communism throughout Latin America, the US tried economic sanctions, assassination attempts and the abortive Bay of Pigs invasion, but all failed to remove him from power.

When Reagan became president he was determined to reassert US power around the world. He supported right-wing governments in El Salvador and Guatemala that were fighting insurrections, and even backed the Contra rebels against the left-wing Sandinista government in Nicaragua. The human costs were high, with 300,000 deaths in Central America in 1975–91.

Captured Cuban exiles after their failed invasion of Cuba, April 1961.

Soviet postage stamp, 1988: 'Perestroika continues the cause of the October Revolution: acceleration, democratization, openness [*glasnost*]'.

Shultz and US Vice-President George H. W. Bush when they first met him in March 1985 for Chernenko's funeral. The prospects for better US-Soviet relations were further enhanced by the absence of major points of contention between the two powers, compared to Vietnam in the 1960s or Africa and the Middle East in the 1970s. Reagan's anti-Communist campaign in Central America did not result in a Soviet response – not least because of Moscow's greater sensitivity to the costs of intervention.

Gorbachev took the initiative. In April 1985 he said he would stop the deployment of intermediate-range nuclear missiles in Eastern Europe and promised to make this permanent if the Americans did the same. In August he announced a temporary moratorium on nuclear tests and suggested the Americans follow his example. Washington declined, in part because of problems of verification but principally because this would have stopped their work on SDI. Then Gorbachev suggested a meeting with Reagan. The November 1985

Ronald Reagan and Mikhail Gorbachev at their first summit meeting, Geneva, 19 November 1985.

ABOVE George Shultz and Soviet foreign minister Eduard Shevardnadze shake hands after signing an agreement on cooperation in space exploration, April 1987.

Geneva summit between Gorbachev and Reagan was friendly and courteous but reached no agreements. Nevertheless, they clearly liked one another and began to develop respect and a readiness to trust each other. All the same, Reagan remained cautious, continuing to approve Weinberger's tough attitude to the Soviet Union.

For the next eleven months the two leaders maintained a regular correspondence on a range of issues, from disarmament to Afghanistan and Nicaragua to human rights, sometimes expressing themselves in direct and blunt style. In the course of their exchanges, Gorbachev made a concession: he would no longer include British and French nuclear arms in the negotiations on intermediate-range nuclear weapons in Europe. As a result, another Reagan-Gorbachev summit took place in Reykjavik in October 1986, at which they deepened their mutual understanding and even came close to reaching agreement to eliminate all their ballistic missiles. The stumbling block, however, was again Reagan's continued commitment to SDI.

Although the Iceland summit did not achieve a breakthrough, it demonstrated a desire to find solutions to mutual problems. It emboldened Shultz and Shevardnadze in the INF talks. The September 1987 agreement removed all intermediate-range weapons from Europe, the so-called 'zero option'. Gorbachev dropped his demand for American abandonment of SDI; his advisers told him that Congress would restrain Reagan's plans, and indeed it did, cutting the SDI

budget by a third. So, at the Washington summit in December 1987, Gorbachev and Reagan signed one of the most significant arms-limitation treaties of the 20th century. The INF Treaty, quickly ratified by the US Senate, resulted in the verified destruction of all ground-launched nuclear missiles with a range of 500–5,500 km (300–3,400 miles) in Europe and Asia – 1,846 Soviet weapons and 846 US weapons. The scale of the achievement fostered public enthusiasm, which was heightened by the hitherto unprecedented sight of a Soviet leader and his wife mingling happily with the American public.

In May 1988 the Soviets began to withdraw their forces from Afghanistan, completed by February 1989. In the following month a US-Soviet deal was signed on South-West Africa: Cuban troops would leave Angola and South African forces would quit Namibia, which would become independent. Gorbachev also settled the long-running frontier dispute with China, accepting the middle of the Ussuri River as their border. In May 1989 he made the first visit to Beijing by a Soviet leader since Khrushchev in the 1950s.

The final Reagan-Gorbachev summit in Moscow in May–June 1988 made real progress towards its goal of a 50 per cent cut in strategic nuclear weapons, but technical difficulties centred on sea- and air-launched Cruise missiles made it impossible to sign a START treaty. The disappointment felt by both leaders was testament to the extent to which East-West relations had been transformed. During the visit Reagan spoke at Moscow State University on what he called the 'bless-ings of democracy and individual freedom and free enterprise',[6] and his words did not lead to tensions. But the strongest indication of the entirely new character of the relationship came with Gorbachev's speech to the UN on 7 December 1988. He declared that ideological differences were disappearing and that 'force and the threat of force can no longer be…instruments of foreign policy'.[7] He then announced that Soviet conventional forces would be cut by 500,000 troops and there would be significant withdrawals from Eastern Europe.

Gorbachev, Shultz and Thatcher all believed that the achieve-ments of 1988 marked the end of the Cold War. Certainly the ideo-logical hostility seemed at an end, and agreement on reducing nuclear weapons had all but been accomplished. Yet Germany was still divided, the Communists remained in power in Eastern Europe, and NATO and the Warsaw Pact faced one another in Central

ABOVE Mikhail Gorbachev arrives in Beijing for a Sino-Soviet summit, 16 May 1989.

OPPOSITE BELOW Ronald Reagan and Mikhail Gorbachev sign the INF Treaty in the White House, 8 December 1987.

National Security Adviser Brent Scowcroft, President George H. W. Bush and Secretary of State James Baker.

Europe: two rival political and social systems still existed. Reagan was succeeded by a new American president after Vice-President George H. W. Bush won the November 1988 election. In February 1989 Bush ordered a major review of US-Soviet relations, which meant that various bilateral talks were suspended; arms negotiations did not resume until September 1989. While the Americans were evaluating the situation, events were overtaking them.

The Soviet bloc witnessed growing dissent towards the Communist authorities. In March 1989 Soviet elections brought defeat for numerous Communist Party functionaries, while nationalists in the Baltic and Caucasian republics as well as a number of Russian liberals and radicals won power. Solidarity pressured the Polish authorities to hold free elections in June, which produced a huge victory for Solidarity. Tension mounted throughout the summer as Moscow pondered whether to permit a non-Communist government in Poland. Eventually a compromise was agreed: Communists would serve as defence and interior ministers while the prime minister would be a non-Communist. In August Tadeusz Mazowiecki became the first non-Communist prime minister in Eastern or Central Europe since 1948. In October Gorbachev's press spokesman, Gennady Gerasimov, announced what he called the 'Frank Sinatra doctrine': each country in the Soviet bloc could 'do it my way'. Confirmation of this more relaxed approach could be seen on 16 June when the Hungarian government permitted its population to commemorate the execution of Imre Nagy, hero of the 1956 uprising. More significant was the Hungarian decision to open its border with Austria in May. As a result, large numbers of East Germans travelled to Hungary and then on to the West. The GDR demanded action by the Hungarians, who restricted movements across their borders. But East Germans then went in huge numbers to the West German embassies in Budapest and Prague. This reached crisis point in August, when a deal was struck allowing these refugees to travel to the West on trains that passed through East Germany.

The crisis for East Germany came just as it reached its fortieth anniversary. As demonstrations for reform spread throughout the

East Germans break through a Hungarian border fence and cross into Austria, 1989.

country, the government had to decide how to respond. A similar movement for reform was emerging in China, centred in Tiananmen Square in Beijing. The Chinese Communist authorities were determined to resist it and in June used tanks to break up the protest. The East Germans possessed the military and police forces to adopt a similarly tough response. They preferred, however, to follow Gorbachev's lead and try to introduce *perestroika*-style reforms under a new leader, Egon Krenz, who replaced Erich Honecker in October. The new government made a mistake in granting the request for freedom of travel by not excluding Berlin (usually given special status). It then compounded the error by declaring that the new regulations would apply immediately: such changes normally had to await ratification by the legislature. Thousands of people quickly assembled at the Berlin Wall. The border guards, under pressure from the crowds, lacked clear instructions but were reluctant to use force. So they decided to open the Wall on the night of 8–9 November, and almost at once people began to tear down the great symbol of East-West division.

Demonstrations during the inter-German summit in Dresden, East Germany, 20 December 1989.

Protests in Tiananmen Square, Beijing, between 15 April and 4 June, known as the June Fourth Movement or Movement for Democracy.

The fall of the Berlin Wall triggered the collapse of Communist regimes across Eastern Europe. Czechoslovakia witnessed a 'Velvet Revolution', as the dissident playwright Vaclav Havel became president in December. The only instance of bloodshed was in Romania, where a violent coup was followed by the execution of President

Slogan on a bus shelter in Wenceslas Square, Prague, following the 'Velvet Revolution' of 1989.

Nicolae Ceausescu and his wife Elena. In 1990 the Communists also lost power in Bulgaria. Unpopular, economically inefficient governments were collapsing under the weight of popular protest. Gorbachev would not send Soviet troops and discouraged the national Communist parties from using force. He was increasingly concerned by his growing domestic problems, and the cost of Soviet aid to these regimes was proving prohibitive: it is estimated that the subsidy in 1981 to Poland alone cost $1 billion. Bush skilfully took the pressure off Gorbachev by not gloating over the changes, and the Gorbachev-Bush summit in Malta in December 1989 displayed a real spirit of cooperation. It also marked the end of the clash between two economic systems, as the Soviets accepted aid that was tied to the condition that they would improve human rights and move towards a market economy. The transformation was staggering – the Soviets and Americans were acting more like allies than adversaries.

In the course of the next year the final Cold War division was removed when German unification was formally ratified in October 1990. Such a development seemed highly improbable even in late 1989, as Gorbachev, Thatcher and French president François Mitterand opposed it. But the West German chancellor Helmut Kohl enlisted the support of the Bush administration, and, as the GDR disintegrated, Mitterand recognized the irresistibility of events. The March 1990 multiparty elections in East Germany gave 48 per cent to Kohl's Christian Democrats (CDU), 22 per cent to the Socialists (SPD) and 16 per cent to the Communists, and the new government agreed to join West Germany. So Gorbachev finally agreed to talks on a united Germany: the 'Two Plus Four' negotiations involved the two German states on domestic issues and the four occupying powers on international questions. By an agreement between Kohl and Gorbachev in July, Germany accepted its existing frontiers, limited its army to 370,000 troops and pledged financial aid for the Soviet withdrawal (this eventually amounted to $9.5 billion). In return, a Soviet-German Friendship Treaty would be signed, Germany would be a full member of NATO and Soviet occupation rights would end. The Final Settlement on Germany of September 1990 accepted the Kohl-Gorbachev accords and formally ended four-power occupation of Germany. All-German elections in December resulted in CDU victory: they won 46 per cent of the vote to the SPD's 33 per cent and the Communists' 10 per cent.

German unification coincided with another major disarmament agreement between NATO and the Warsaw Pact – the Conventional Forces in Europe (CFE, formerly known as MBFR talks) Treaty of November 1990. It applied to military equipment rather than numbers of troops. Thirty-four nations gathered in Paris to confirm the agreement between the sixteen NATO and six Warsaw Pact members that each alliance would be allowed a total of 20,000 tanks, no more than 13,300 of them belonging to any one country. This international summit – sometimes referred to as the peace conference of the Cold War – also produced the Charter of Paris, a declaration of democratic rights and individual freedoms.

The political developments of 1990 marked a decisive turning point. If 1988 saw the end of the ideological struggle between East and West and 1989 witnessed the collapse of Communist rule in Eastern Europe, then 1990 confirmed the irrevocable shift by settling the German question. Postwar disagreements about Germany, after all, had precipitated the US-Soviet division. The Kremlin was now preoccupied with the internal disintegration of the USSR, whose fifteen republics sought greater autonomy. Ukraine, Georgia and Armenia pressed for full independence, but perhaps the most surprising advocate of independence was the Russian republic, led by Boris Yeltsin (appointed president in May 1990 and then elected in June 1991). The most explosive nationalism was displayed in the Baltic states of Lithuania, Latvia and Estonia, countries which had

ABOVE Crowds in front of the Berlin Wall and the Brandenburg Gate, 1989.

BELOW One of many road signs indicating where Germany and Europe were divided until December 1989.

enjoyed independence in the interwar years and wished to reverse their absorption in 1939 by the Soviets.

Gorbachev was reluctant to lose integral parts of the USSR. Instead, he proposed a 'Union of Sovereign States' that would allow its members substantial autonomy. However, this concession was intolerable for the hardliners. The KGB chief Vladimir Kryuchkov and his allies – the premier Valentin Pavlov, deputy head of the Defence Council Oleg Baklanov, and defence minister Dmitry Yazov – tried to seize power in August 1991. Yeltsin rallied tens of thousands of Muscovites to resist them, and the coup failed when the majority of the security forces refused to act against these citizens. Yeltsin's victory confirmed the hollowness of both Gorbachev's position and the Soviet state. Power now lay with the leaders of the various republics and Yeltsin in particular. On 8 December 1991 the presidents of Russia, Ukraine and Belorussia (Belarus) unilaterally dissolved the USSR and replaced it with a Commonwealth of Independent States (CIS). On 21 December all the other republics, except the Baltics and Georgia, joined the CIS. Recognizing reality, Gorbachev resigned on 25 December, and the following day the Soviet Union ceased to exist. One last disarmament treaty was signed by the USSR on 31 July 1991, shortly before its collapse: in the START agreement, Washington and Moscow pledged to halve their joint stockpile of nuclear warheads to about 6,000 by 1998.

The disappearance of the Soviet Union was the final confirmation that the Cold War was over. Scholars continue to debate why the conflict ended in the way and at the time it did. Supporters of Ronald Reagan claim that it was due to his determination to increase American defence spending to such a level that the Soviets could not compete and would be obliged to seek agreements that would reduce their military costs. George H. W. Bush is also credited for his conciliatory approach. Most historians, however, consider Gorbachev's role as decisive. The Soviet economy in the 1980s suffered from severe problems, but most analysts thought it was capable of sustaining the arms race with Washington, even though this would have brought further deterioration. What was vital, these writers argue, was Gorbachev's decision not to do this but, instead, to seek accommodation with the West. Deals with the Americans would allow him to reduce the huge costs of supporting his allies and funding the military and

Boris Yeltsin, Russia's first elected president (June 1991), speaking in 1994.

Russian soldier loyal to the coup leaders on his tank in Red Square, Moscow, August 1991.

so permit him to concentrate on reforming and revitalizing the entire Soviet political and economic system. He was prepared to offer concessions to achieve this, and all the major breakthroughs came as a result of concessions made by Gorbachev. These arguments are very persuasive, but without American pressure it is unlikely that change would have been as far-reaching. In truth, the Cold War ended because of the complementary contributions of Gorbachev, Reagan and Bush, fulfilling the desires of the overwhelming majority on both sides of the East-West divide.

Chapter 7

Legacies: Triumph of the West?

The disappearance of Communism as a significant force and the collapse of the Soviet Union seemed a clear victory for the West, which had won both the geopolitical struggle and the competition between the two visions of politics and economics. The newly independent states of Eastern Europe and former republics of the Soviet Union adopted Western models. The world appeared to be changing for the better – even in Africa, where Nelson Mandela was released from prison in February 1990 and then elected as the first black president of South Africa in 1994.

The spread of its values and culture around the world encouraged American self-confidence, which was reinforced by the country's overwhelming military dominance – the French coined the term 'hyperpower'. Some Americans were triumphalist – in 'The End of History?' (1989), Francis Fukuyama claimed that the defeat of Communism signalled the end of all other serious ideological competitors to capitalism and liberal democracy. Despite the international reach of US power, foreign affairs came to play a diminishing role in American domestic politics: it hardly featured in the 1992, 1996 and 2000 presidential elections, and the State Department closed thirty embassies and twenty-five USIA libraries. Yet defence expenditure, although reduced, remained high ($325 billion in 1995). In the absence of Cold War tensions, Americans increasingly focused on economic issues.

As the United States and other countries pursued economic opportunities in the more open world of the 1990s, there was a

Nelson Mandela at a rally in Wembley Stadium, London, April 1990.

OPPOSITE The ruins of the south tower of the World Trade Center, 11 September 2001.

Chinese man holding a
bottle of Coca-Cola poses
on the Great Wall,
December 1983.

growth in international connections – a development that came to be
known as globalization, loosely defined as the free movement of
ideas, people, trade and finance. The process had begun as far back as
1958 when currency convertibility allowed money to circulate more
freely, a trend that increased with the emergence of floating currencies in the 1970s. In the 1980s the liberalization of trade (world trade
grew by 48 per cent during 1981–91) and the communications revolution that brought computers and the internet opened up the world
still more. But it was the end of the Cold War that marked the decisive

shift, as the restrictions on exchanges with East European states and the Soviet Union disappeared. The United States dominated this globalized world, disproving the prediction that Japan would become the world's largest economy. The biggest beneficiaries proved to be the Chinese, though this would not be clear until a decade later. Americans had cultivated better relations with China as a counterweight to the Soviet Union, thereby encouraging the Chinese to be more engaged with the rest of the world. By stages after 1978 the Chinese opened up their economy to capitalist enterprise and embarked on an export programme, and this was generating double-digit growth rates by the beginning of the 21st century.

The revival of nationalism also contributed to the demise of the Cold War. East Europeans asserted pride in their own nations; Soviet republics including Ukraine, Georgia and the Baltic states gained their independence. But this, in turn, released deep ethnic and religious divisions within and between countries. Sometimes these were resolved peacefully, as in Czechoslovakia, which became two sovereign states in the so-called 'Velvet Divorce' of 1993. In Yugoslavia, however, the resurgence of long-suppressed enmities led to bloody civil war. As a federal state it was made up of six republics – Serbia, Croatia, Bosnia-Herzegovina, Macedonia, Slovenia and Montenegro – and two autonomous regions, Vojvodina and Kosovo. After 1989,

UN armoured vehicle in Sarajevo during the ceasefire, April 1994.

civil war broke out between the Serbs and Croats and the conflict eventually spread to Bosnia and Kosovo, which led to military intervention by NATO in 1999 followed by UN administration.

The most disruptive post-Cold War development was the emergence of violently anti-American Islamism. Its roots lay in the Iranian Revolution of 1979, but it was deeply affected by the way globalization was spreading American culture and influence even into the Middle East. Osama Bin Laden, a wealthy Saudi Arabian, established a network called al-Qaeda. On 11 September 2001 the group hijacked four American passenger aircraft and crashed two of them into the World Trade Center in New York and another into the Pentagon, killing nearly 3,000 people.

The growing importance of this terrorist threat, as well as the ethnic, religious and tribal tensions that have produced 'failed states', led many commentators to argue that the era of great power rivalry was at an end, and the post-Cold War fate of Russia seemed to confirm this judgment. Political instability and economic chaos left it subdued in the 1990s, with limited international power. Its leaders could do little to stop its neighbours from joining Western institutions, and the majority sought membership of NATO and the European Union. Yet Russia still possessed a large nuclear arsenal, and when Vladimir Putin became Russian president in 1999, he began to reassert his country's global status. Meanwhile, the Chinese have steadily built up their military strength and behaved more assertively in Asia, becoming involved in territorial disputes with Japan.

At the beginning of the second decade of the 21st century, the end of the Cold War looks much less like a triumph for the West.

Resources

Chronology

1917 Bolshevik Revolution in Russia (November)

1919 Creation of the Communist International (Comintern)

1920 US refuses to recognize Bolshevik government

1922 Creation of Soviet Union

1933 US recognizes Soviet Union

1939 Nazi-Soviet Pact (August); German invasion of Poland (1 September); Britain and France declare war against Germany (3 September)

1940–41 Soviet-Finnish War

1941 German invasion of Soviet Union (22 June); Japanese attack on US at Pearl Harbor, Hawaii (7 December)

1941–45 Big Three (Britain, United States and Soviet Union) Alliance against Germany

1943 Tehran conference of Big Three leaders (Churchill, Roosevelt and Stalin) (November)

1945 Yalta conference of Big Three leaders (Churchill, Roosevelt and Stalin) (February); Potsdam conference of Big Three leaders (Churchill/Attlee, Truman and Stalin) (July–August); publication of George Orwell's *Animal Farm* (August)

1946 George Kennan's 'Long Telegram' (February); Winston Churchill's 'Iron Curtain' speech in Fulton, Missouri (March)

1947 Harry Truman's speech to Congress on Truman Doctrine (March); George Marshall's speech at Harvard University announces US aid (June), leading to Marshall Plan (1948–52); anonymous (George Kennan) article enunciates US containment policy (July)

1948–49 Berlin blockade (June 1948–May 1949)

1949 North Atlantic Treaty signed, creating NATO (April); publication of George Orwell's *1984* (June); Communist victory in China (October)

1950 Senator Joe McCarthy's speech claims Communist spies in US State Department (February); North Korean attack on South Korea (25 June)

1953 Korean War armistice (July)

1954 French defeat by Vietminh at Dien Bien Phu (May)

1955 Germany rearmed and member of NATO (May); creation of Warsaw Pact (May); Geneva summit of Big Four leaders (Eisenhower, Eden, Bulganin and Faure) (July); Khrushchev emerges as Soviet leader (July)

1956 Elvis Presley releases *Heartbreak Hotel* (January); Suez crisis (October–November); Hungarian Uprising (November)

1958–61 Crises over Berlin

1962 Cuban missile crisis (October)

1963 Nuclear Test Ban Treaty (August); Kennedy assassination (November)

1964 Release of Stanley Kubrick's film *Dr Strangelove* (January); Beatles conquer the United States

1965 US combat troops enter Vietnam

1968 Tet offensive in Vietnam (January–September); anti-war protests grow; Nuclear Non-Proliferation Treaty (July)

1969–72 Détente

1972 Nixon visits China (February); SALT I (Strategic Arms Limitation Talks) agreement (May)

1973 Yom Kippur War (October); oil prices rise by 70 per cent

1974 Nixon resigns (August)

1975 Helsinki Accords (August)

1979 Islamic Revolution in Iran (February); oil prices double; SALT II agreement (June); US embassy hostages taken in Tehran (November); Soviet invasion of Afghanistan (December)

1980 US boycott of Moscow Olympics (July)

1982 Publication of Raymond Briggs's *When the Wind Blows*

1983 Reagan's 'evil empire' speech (March); Soviets shoot down KAL 007 (September); NATO exercise 'Able Archer' (November); deployment of Cruise and Pershing missiles in Western Europe (November)

1985 Geneva summit (Reagan and Gorbachev) (November)

1986 Reykjavik summit (Reagan and Gorbachev) (October)

1987 INF (Intermediate Nuclear Forces) agreement (September)

1988 Moscow summit (Reagan and Gorbachev) (May–June)

1989 East European revolutions; fall of Berlin Wall (November)

1990 Unification of Germany

1991 START (Strategic Arms Reduction Talks) Treaty (July); collapse of the Soviet Union (December)

Notes

Chapter 1 Origins: 1917–1945

1 Quoted in Tzouliadis, Tim, *The Forsaken: An American Tragedy in Stalin's Russia* (New York: 2008), p. 6
2 Palmer, A. Mitchell, 'The Case Against the Reds', *Forum* 63 (1920), pp. 173–85, quoted in Hanhimaki, Jussi M. and Westad, Odd Arne (eds), *The Cold War: A History in Documents and Eyewitness Accounts* (Oxford: 2003), pp. 6–8
3 Churchill to Roosevelt on 7 March 1942, in Churchill, Winston S., *The Second World War*, 6 vols (London: 1951), vol. IV, p. 293
4 Truman, Harry S., *Year of Decisions* (New York: 1965), pp. 96–99

Chapter 2 Confrontation: 1945–1950

1 'X' (George Kennan), 'The Sources of Soviet Conduct', *Foreign Affairs* (1947), pp. 566–82
2 Churchill, Winston, 'The Sinews of Peace', in Churchill, Randolph S. (ed.), *The Sinews of Peace: Post-War Speeches by Winston S. Churchill* (London: 1948), pp. 83–105
3 The text of Byrnes's speech is in *Department of State Bulletin*, vol. XV, no. 376 (15 September 1946), pp. 496–501
4 George Marshall's address to Harvard University, 5 June 1947, quoted in Hanhimaki, Jussi M. and Westad, Odd Arne (eds), *The Cold War: A History in Documents and Eyewitness Accounts* (Oxford: 2003), p. 122
5 Truman's Special Message to Congress, 17 March 1948, available at www.trumanlibrary.org/publicpapers/index.php (accessed 1 June 2010)
6 Brandt, Willy, *My Road to Berlin* (London: 1960), pp. 184–98, quoted in Hanhimaki, Jussi M. and Westad, Odd Arne (eds), *The Cold War: A History in Documents and Eyewitness Accounts* (Oxford: 2003), pp. 98–99
7 *Pravda*, 26 February 1949, quoted in Mayers, David, *The Ambassadors and America's Soviet Policy* (New York and Oxford: 1995), p. 289, n. 2

Chapter 3 Crises and Neuroses: 1950–1962

1 Eisenhower press conference, 7 April 1954, available at www.presidency.ucsb.edu (accessed 27 January 2011)

2 Khrushchev to Western ambassadors at the Polish embassy, Moscow, 18 November 1956, quoted in *Time*, 26 November 1956, available at www.time.com (accessed 27 January 2011)

Chapter 4 Cooperation and Protest: 1962–1972

1 Kennedy's commencement address at American University, 10 June 1963, available at www.presidency.ucsb.edu (accessed 1 September 2010)
2 Johnson's Special Message to Congress on US policy in South-East Asia, 5 August 1964, available at www.presidency.ucsb.edu (accessed 27 January 2011)
3 Quoted in Walker, Martin, *The Cold War and the Making of the Modern World* (London: 1993), p. 189
4 Guevara, Che, *Guerrilla Warfare: A Method* (1964), quoted in Hanhimaki, Jussi M. and Westad, Odd Arne (eds), *The Cold War: A History in Documents and Eyewitness Accounts* (Oxford: 2003), p. 399
5 KGB report, 7 June 1962, quoted in Hanhimaki, Jussi M. and Westad, Odd Arne (eds), *The Cold War: A History in Documents and Eyewitness Accounts* (Oxford: 2003), p. 433

Chapter 5 Bleak Midwinter: 1972–1983

1 Kissinger to Gromyko, May 1972, quoted in Hanhimaki, Jussi M. and Westad, Odd Arne (eds), *The Cold War: A History in Documents and Eyewitness Accounts* (Oxford: 2003), p. 231
2 Sadat's address to the Knessett, 20 November 1977, available at www.jewishvirtuallibrary.org (accessed 27 January 2011)
3 Carter's State of the Union address, 23 January 1980, available at www.presidency.ucsb.edu (accessed 27 January 2011)
4 Lech Walesa in talks with Polish Communist Party officials, 23 August 1980, quoted in Hanhimaki, Jussi M. and Westad, Odd Arne (eds), *The Cold War: A History in Documents and Eyewitness Accounts* (Oxford: 2003), p. 569
5 Reagan's speech to the annual convention of the National Association of Evangelicals, Orlando, Florida, 8 March 1983, available at www.presidency.ucsb.edu (accessed 27 January 2011)
6 Reagan's address to the nation, 5 September 1983, available at www.presidency.ucsb.edu (accessed 27 January 2011)

Chapter 6 Endings: 1983–1991

1 Reagan's speech to the annual convention of the National Association of Evangelicals, Orlando, Florida, 8 March 1983, available at www.presidency.ucsb.edu (accessed 27 January 2011)
2 Reagan, Ronald, *An American Life* (London: 1990), pp. 588, 589
3 Reagan, Ronald, *An American Life* (London: 1990), p. 589
4 Reagan, Ronald, *An American Life* (London: 1990), p. 605
5 Shultz, George P., *Triumph and Turmoil* (New York: 1993), p. 702
6 Reagan's remarks at question-and-answer session with students and faculty at Moscow State University, 31 May 1988, available at www.presidency.ucsb.edu (accessed 27 January 2011)
7 Gorbachev's speech to the UN, 7 December 1988, excerpts available at www.wilsoncenter.org/coldwarfiles/files/documents/1988-1107. Gorbachev.pdf (accessed 27 January 2011)

Further Reading

Gaddis, John Lewis, *The Cold War* (London: 2005)
Herring, George C., *From Colony to Superpower: U.S. Foreign Relations since 1776* (New York and Oxford: 2008)
Leffler, Melvyn P. and Westad, Odd Arne (eds), *The Cambridge History of the Cold War*, 3 vols (Cambridge: 2010)
Reynolds, David, *Britannia Overruled: British Policy and World Power in the Twentieth Century*, 2nd edn (London and New York: 2000)
Reynolds, David, *One World Divisible: A Global History since 1945* (London and New York: 2000)
Soutou, Georges-Henri, *La Guerre de Cinquante Ans* (Paris: 2001)
Walker, Martin, *The Cold War and the Making of the Modern World* (London: 1993)
Whitfield, Stephen J., *The Culture of the Cold War*, 2nd edn (Baltimore: 1996)
Zubok, Vladislav M., *A Failed Empire: The Soviet Union in the Cold War from Stalin to Gorbachev* (Chapel Hill: 2007)

Translations and Transcriptions of the Documents

1 'Agit Plakat No. 2' ('Agit Poster No. 2'), a Soviet political propaganda poster by Kaplan and Fridkin. It explains in Ukrainian the importance of changing work habits as part of the First Five-Year Plan (1928–32), a series of industrial targets designed by the Stalinist regime to build up heavy industry in the Soviet Union. Lithograph, 147 x 71.5 cm (58 x 28 in), probably early 1930s.

2 Membership card of the Communist Party of the USSR, 1942.

3 'How to Survive An Atomic Bomb', an advertisement sponsored by the Mutual of Omaha insurance company, 1951.

> **How to Survive an Atomic Bomb...**   January 1951
>
> Whatever your attitude toward use of the atomic bomb, *you must live with the fact that it exists.* You must know how to *protect yourself* as much as you can against it. As with flood, fire or other catastrophes, certain common sense rules apply. The wise citizen of the atomic era will memorize them so thoroughly that their use would be almost instinctive.
>
> **IMMEDIATE ACTION**, should a surprise atomic attack occur, could mean the difference between life and death. First sign of an atomic explosion would be an intensely bright light. You must *resist the impulse to look toward the source of this burning brightness.* Rather, use the next one or two seconds for quick protective action.
>
> **DROP TO THE GROUND** instantly if you are in the open or less than a few steps from protection, such as a tree or the corner of a building. Your immediate reaction must be to *shield yourself from the flash of brilliance.* If indoors, drop to the floor with your back to the window, or crawl behind or beneath a protecting piece of furniture.

CURL UP in such a way as to shield your face, neck, hands and arms. Unless you happen to be close to the immediate area of the bomb, *your greatest danger would be from flash burns* which could seriously damage exposed areas of skin. Hold this curled up position for at least 10 seconds.

THERMAL RADIATION...the burning brightness...can be dangerous as far as two miles from the point of origin. *But the rays travel in straight lines.* So if you instantly shelter yourself from these rays, you may avoid serious burns. At least, protect yourself with your own body...let your back take the brunt of the rays. Clothing...especially light clothing...can usually prevent rays from reaching your body.

BE ALERT FOR THE BLAST WAVE which spreads outward for as much as a minute or more *after* the explosion. If on the street, press close to a building so that you are sheltered from breaking glass or falling debris. If indoors, keep away from windows...they may shatter. The safest place within a building is likely to be against an interior partition or in the basement.

WORK IN ADVANCE TO AVOID PANIC. This can best be done by working with your local civilian defense organization. *Study the fund of information available on defensive measures.* By careful planning, your community can be prepared to hold death and destruction to a minimum.

4 The first and last pages of President Truman's address to a joint session of Congress, 12 March 1947, which became known as the Truman Doctrine.

ADDRESS OF THE PRESIDENT OF THE UNITED STATES DELIVERED BEFORE A JOINT SESSION OF THE SENATE AND THE HOUSE OF REPRESENTATIVES, RECOMMENDING ASSISTANCE TO GREECE AND TURKEY

MARCH 12, 1947.—Referred to the Committee on Foreign Affairs, and ordered to be printed

Mr. President, Mr. Speaker, Members of the Congress of the United States:

The gravity of the situation which confronts the world today necessitates my appearance before a joint session of the Congress.

The foreign policy and the national security of this country are involved.

One aspect of the present situation, which I wish to present to you at this time for your consideration and decision, concerns Greece and Turkey.

The United States has received from the Greek Government an urgent appeal for financial and economic assistance. Preliminary reports from the American Economic Mission now in Greece and reports from the American Ambassador in Greece corroborate the statement of the Greek Government that assistance is imperative if Greece is to survive as a free nation.

I do not believe that the American people and the Congress wish to turn a deaf ear to the appeal of the Greek Government.

Greece is not a rich country. Lack of sufficient natural resources has always forced the Greek people to work hard to make both ends meet. Since 1940, this industrious and peace-loving country has suffered invasion, 4 years of cruel enemy occupation, and bitter internal strife.

When forces of liberation entered Greece they found that the retreating Germans had destroyed virtually all the railways, roads,...

...consideration the maximum amount of relief assistance which would be furnished to Greece out of the $350,000,000 which I recently requested that the Congress authorize for the prevention of starvation and suffering in countries devastated by the war.

In addition to funds, I ask the Congress to authorize the detail of American civilian and military personnel to Greece and Turkey, at the request of those countries, to assist in the tasks of reconstruction, and for the purpose of supervising the use of such financial and material assistance as may be furnished.
I recommend that authority also be provided for the instruction and training of selected Greek and Turkish personnel.

Finally, I ask that the Congress provide authority which will permit the speediest and most effective use, in terms of needed commodities, supplies, and equipment, of such funds as may be authorized.

If further funds, or further authority, should be needed for purposes indicated in this message, I shall not hesitate to bring the situation before the Congress. On this subject the executive and legislative branches of the Government must work together.

This is a serious course upon which we embark.

I would not recommend it except that the alternative is much more serious.

The United States contributed $341,000,000,000 toward winning World War II. This is an investment in world freedom and world peace.

The assistance that I am recommending for Greece and Turkey amounts to little more than one-tenth of 1 percent of this investment. It is only common sense that we should safeguard this investment and make sure that it was not in vain.

The seeds of totalitarian regimes are nurtured by misery and want. They spread and grow in the evil soil of poverty and strife. They reach their full growth when the hope of a people for a better life has died.

We must keep that hope alive.

The free peoples of the world look to us for support in maintaining their freedoms.

If we falter in our leadership, we may endanger the peace of the world–and we shall surely endanger the welfare of our own Nation.

Great responsibilities have been placed upon us by the swift movement of events.

I am confident that the Congress will face these responsibilities squarely.

HARRY S. TRUMAN.
THE WHITE HOUSE, *March 12, 1947.*

5 Anti-Reagan protesters' poster, London, June 1984.

WANTED
For crimes against humanity and
ENDANGERING WORLD PEACE

REAGAN ON TRIAL

THURSDAY 7th JUNE 1984
FRIENDS HOUSE, EUSTON ROAD NW1
(Doors open 6.00 pm. Exhibitions, Stalls, Snacks.
TRIAL STARTS PROMPTLY 6.30 pm. Tickets: £1.00)

PANEL OF JUDGES to include JOHN PLATTS-MILLS QC
FOR THE PROSECUTION: LORD GIFFORD QC
EXPERT WITNESSES from the regions to be called to give
evidence

Sponsored by: LIBERATION, Grenada Committee for Human
Rights, Nicaragua Solidarity Campaign, El Salvador Solidarity
Campaign, Chile Solidarity Campaign, CARILA, NICA,
Committee for the Defence of Democratic Rights in Turkey,
Solidarity Committee for Trade Union Rights and Democracy in
Turkey, Philippines Support Group, Britain Grenada Friendship
Society, Palestine Co-ordinating Committee, Committee for the
Release of Political Prisoners in Kenya, Namibia Support
Committee, General Union of Palestine Students

6 Chinese-language illustrated version of *Animal Farm* (1945) by George
Orwell, probably published in 1949–50 (scenes 13–16). The book reflects
events leading up to and during the Stalin era before the Second World War.

7 Spanish-language comic, *El Despertar* ('The Awakening'), about Castro's revolution in Cuba, produced by the US government, probably in July 1967.

> We are at the beginning of January 1959…Cuba has liberated itself from the tyranny of Fulgencio Batista. Pepe Cuadros and Mateo Vazquez, sons of local rural families, return to their native village…

> …Where, full of joy, they are reunited with Blanca Vazquez, Mateo's sister and Pepe's sweetheart.

> She says: 'Welcome, my two heroes!'

> He says: 'We will all have our own farms!'

8 'The Free World Speaks', an illustrated account of East-West confrontation produced by the US government, probably 1951–52.

> After the war, the Allies agreed on four-power control of Germany. The United States, Great Britain and France worked for a unified, democratic Germany. Berlin, an island in the Soviet zone, also came under four-power administration.

> Soviet authorities devised countless means to split East and West Germany. In Berlin they resorted to blocking all traffic by rail or highway.

> The United States, Britain and France refused to yield to Soviet pressure. They found a solution – a gigantic airlift that would fly food and supplies into the blockaded city. Result: the USSR lifted the blockade!

> Soviet-occupied Austria was sealed off from the Free World and, in violation of treaties, the Danube River – a great water highway to Vienna and Central Europe – was blocked to free international commerce.

THE IRON CURTAIN CAME DOWN

Following the victory over Nazism, men and women of many
nations hoped they could learn to know the Russian people in
peace time. They were disappointed. An impenetrable Iron
Curtain kept the free people out and the Russians locked in.

Radio broadcasts from the Voice of America, the BBC and other
stations in the Free World were jammed. Soviet leaders knew that
their power depended on keeping the truth from their people.

The Soviet Union, through its radio and press, and its puppet
agitators, poured out a flood of lies against its former allies.

9 President Truman's letter to Senator Richard Russell, 9 August 1945.

> August 9, 1945
> Dear Dick:
>
> I read your telegram of August seventh with a lot of interest.
> I know that Japan is a terribly cruel and uncivilized nation in
> warfare but I can't bring myself to believe that, because they are
> beasts, we should ourselves act in the same manner.
> For myself, I certainly regret the necessity of wiping out whole
> populations because of the "pigheadedness" of the leaders of a
> nation and, for your information, I am not going to do it unless
> it is absolutely necessary. It is my opinion that after the Russians
> enter into war the Japanese will very shortly fold up.
> My object is to save as many American lives as possible but I also
> have a humane feeling for the women and children in Japan.
>
> Sincerely yours,
> HARRY S. TRUMAN
>
> Honorable Richard B. Russell
> Winder
> Georgia

10 Map of Communist advances in East Asia, 14 November 1950. On 7 April 1954 President Eisenhower popularized the 'domino theory' to describe the Communist threat: the idea that one nation 'going Communist' would start a chain reaction in the region.

China's entry into Korean war may be only a diversion, with French Indo-China as real goal for conquest. Red-held Korea would point dagger at Japan. Chinese invasion of Korea is matched by intensified campaign in Indo-China.

Invasion of Tibet may be move to solidify Red China's Indian-border defenses.

Indo-China is the key to southeast Asia. If Reds take over, Burma, Thailand, Malaya and perhaps Indonesia may go down under communism – either by military conquest or internal revolt.

Chinese Reds have not lost hope of seizing Formosa from Nationalists. If they do, they pierce General MacArthur's Japan-Philippines defense arc, posing threat to Okinawa and Philippines.

Communist-held Indo-China would also put Reds on flank of the Philippines.

Sources of Illustrations

a = above, b = below, l = left, r = right
LoC: Library of Congress, Washington, D.C.;
NARA: The U.S. National Archives and Records
Administration, Maryland

1 Marc Charmet/The Art Archive; 2–3 Jacques
Langevin/Sygma/Corbis; 4–5 Corbis; 6 Bettmann/
Corbis; 7 Keystone Pictures USA/Alamy;
8 Tretyakov Gallery, Moscow; 9 William Gottlieb/
Corbis; 10 Stalin Museum, Batumi; 11 Private
collection; 12a LoC; 12b Library of the London
School of Economics and Political Science;
13 LoC; 14 Ivan Vasilyevich Simakov; 15 George
Grantham Bain Collection/LoC; 16a Bettmann/
Corbis; 16b LoC; 17 Imperial War Museum,
London; 18, 19 Dr Harry Bakwin and Dr Ruth
Morris Bakwin Soviet Posters Collection, Special
Collections Research Center, University of Chicago
Library; 20 NARA; 21a Warner Bros./The Kobal
Collection; 21b British Museum, London; 22a, 23a
NARA; 22–23b Zbyszko Siemaszko; 24 NARA;
25 U.S. Coast Guard, Washington, D.C.; 26
Michael Nicholson/Corbis; 27 U.S. Naval Institute,
Maryland; 28 Corbis; 29a People's History Museum,
Manchester; 29b Fred Ramage/Keystone Features/
Getty Images; 30a Hulton-Deutsch Collection/
Corbis; 30b akg-images; 31 George Skadding/
Time Life Pictures/Getty Images; 32 U.S. Air Force;
33a U.S. Army; 33b LoC; 34 NARA; 35a U.S. Army;
35b Swim Ink 2, LLC/Corbis; 36 Gamma-Keystone/
Getty Images; 37a U.S. Air Force; 37b Australian
War Memorial, Canberra (REL31117); 38, 39a
NARA; 39b Bettmann/Corbis; 40 British Museum,
London; 41a NARA; 41b British Museum, London;
43 North Korea International Documentation
Project/Wilson Center, Washington, D.C.; 44a
NARA; 44b U.S. Army; 45 NARA; 46 Museum für
Gestaltung, Zurich; 47a NARA; 47b Bettmann/
Corbis; 48a Red Channels, 22 June 1950; 48bl LoC;
48br Warner Bros. Entertainment, Inc.; 49l NARA;
49ar American Legion Library, Indianapolis;
49br NARA; 50 U.S. Air Force; 51l NARA; 51r
Bettmann/Corbis; 52l, 52r, 53 U.S. Department of
Energy; 54 Bettmann/Corbis; 55l Hulton-Deutsch
Collection/Corbis; 55r LoC; 56 Bettmann/Corbis;
57 University of Arkansas/U.S. Army; 58–59 Dean
Conger/Corbis; 60a NSSDC/NASA; 60b British
Museum, London; 61 Major Steve Heyser/U.S.
Air Force; 62a Cecil Stoughton/John F. Kennedy
Presidential Library and Museum, Boston;
62b, 63l Bettmann/Corbis; 63r Hawk Films
Production/Columbia/The Kobal Collection;
65 Heinz-Jürgen Göttert/DPA/Corbis; 66a U.S.
Air Force; 66b Arnold Newman/White House
Press Office, Washington, D.C.; 67a Express

Newspapers/Getty Images; 67b LoC; 68 Howard
Sochurek/Time Life Pictures/Getty Images;
69, 70, 71 NARA; 72a Australian War Memorial,
Canberra (CUN:66:0376:VN); 72b Smithsonian
American Art Museum, Washington, D.C.;
73 NARA; 75 Jack Burlot/Sygma/Corbis; 76 Libor
Hajsky/EPA/Corbis; 77a Pierre Boulat/Time Life
Pictures/Getty Images; 77b U.S. Army; 78 Richard
Nixon Presidential Library and Museum,
California; 79, 81 Bettmann/Corbis; 82 AFP/Getty
Images; 83 Richard Nixon Presidential Library
and Museum, California; 84–85a U.S. Army;
84b Bettmann/Corbis; 85b U.S. Department of
Defense, Washington, D.C.; 86 ClassicStock/
Alamy; 88 Bettmann/Corbis; 89l Hulton-Deutsch
Collection/Corbis; 89r Bettmann/Corbis;
90 Keystone/Getty Images; 91l U.S. Navy; 91r Sgt
Kevin Gruenwald/U.S. Air Force; 92 Richard Nixon
Presidential Library and Museum, California;
93 Bettmann/Corbis; 94 Gerald R. Ford Presidential
Library and Museum, Michigan; 95 Jimmy Carter
Library and Museum, Atlanta; 96a Henri Bureau/
Sygma/Corbis; 96b Johnson Space Center/NASA;
97 George Chernilevsky; 98 LoC; 99a Phillip
Maiwald; 99b Bettmann/Corbis; 100 Pascal
Manoukian/Sygma/Corbis; 101 U.S. Air Force;
102 Tony Comiti/Corbis; 103 Trinity Mirror/
Mirrorpix/Alamy; 104, 105 Bettmann/Corbis;
106 Ronald Reagan Presidential Foundation and
Library, California; 107 U.S. Air Force; 108 David
Brauchli/Reuters/Corbis; 110 U.S. Department of
Defense, Washington, D.C.; 111 Peter Turnley/
Corbis; 112 Three Lions/Getty Images; 113a LoC;
113b Ronald Reagan Presidential Foundation and
Library, California; 114a Peter Turnley/Corbis;
114b Ronald Reagan Presidential Foundation and
Library, California; 115 Peter Turnley/Corbis;
116 David Valdez/Time Life Pictures/Getty
Images; 117 Reuters/Corbis; 118–119b Bernard
Bisson/Sygma/Corbis; 119a Durand-Langevin/
Sygma/Corbis; 120 Paul Glendell/Alamy;
121a Caro/Alamy; 121b Doris Antony; 122 Wally
McNamee/Corbis; 123 Peter Turnley/Corbis;
124 Aristede Economopoulos/Star Ledger/Corbis;
125 Peter Turnley/Corbis; 126 Owen Franken/
Corbis; 127 Patrick Chauvel/Sygma/Corbis

Facsimile documents

1 Dr Harry Bakwin and Dr Ruth Morris Bakwin
Soviet Posters Collection, Special Collections
Research Center, University of Chicago Library;
2, 3 LoC; 4 NARA; 5 LoC; 6, 7, 8 NARA;
9 Harry S. Truman Library and Museum,
Missouri; 10 Bettmann/Corbis

Index

Page numbers in *italic* refer to illustrations